# Tort
# Reform

**POINT COUNTERPOINT**

# Tort
# Reform

## Paul Ruschmann, J.D.

SERIES CONSULTING EDITOR
### Alan Marzilli, M.A., J.D.

CHELSEA HOUSE
P U B L I S H E R S
A Haights Cross Communications Company ®

Philadelphia

## CHELSEA HOUSE PUBLISHERS

VP, NEW PRODUCT DEVELOPMENT Sally Cheney
DIRECTOR OF PRODUCTION Kim Shinners
CREATIVE MANAGER Takeshi Takahashi
MANUFACTURING MANAGER Diann Grasse

### Staff for TORT REFORM

EXECUTIVE EDITOR Lee Marcott
EDITORIAL ASSISTANT Carla Greenberg
PHOTO EDITOR Sarah Bloom
PRODUCTION EDITOR Bonnie Cohen
SERIES AND COVER DESIGNER Keith Trego
LAYOUT 21st Century Publishing and Communications, Inc.

A Haights Cross Communications ⌖ Company ®

http://www.chelseahouse.com

First Printing

1 3 5 7 9 8 6 4 2

Library of Congress Cataloging-in-Publication Data

Ruschmann, Paul.
    Tort reform/Paul Ruschmann.
       p. cm.—(Point/counterpoint)
    Includes bibliographical references and index.
    ISBN 0-7910-8645-3 (hardcover)
    1. Torts—United States. 2. Actions and defenses—United States. 3. Law reform—
United States. I. Title. II. Point-counterpoint (Philadelphia, Pa.)
    KF1251.R87 2005
    346.7303—dc22
                                                                2005003268

All links and web addresses were checked and verified to be correct at the time of
publication. Because of the dynamic nature of the web, some addresses and links
may have changed since publication and may no longer be valid.

# CONTENTS

# Foreword
**Alan Marzilli, M.A., J.D.**
**Durham, North Carolina**

The debates presented in POINT/COUNTERPOINT are among the most interesting and controversial in contemporary American society, but studying them is more than an academic activity. They affect every citizen; they are the issues that today's leaders debate and tomorrow's will decide. The reader may one day play a central role in resolving them.

Why study both sides of the debate? It's possible that the reader will not yet have formed any opinion at all on the subject of this volume—but this is unlikely. It is more likely that the reader will already hold an opinion, probably a strong one, and very probably one formed without full exposure to the arguments of the other side. It is rare to hear an argument presented in a balanced way, and it is easy to form an opinion on too little information; these books will help to fill in the informational gaps that can never be avoided. More important, though, is the practical function of the series: Skillful argumentation requires a thorough knowledge of *both* sides—though there are seldom only two, and only by knowing what an opponent is likely to assert can one form an articulate response.

Perhaps more important is that listening to the other side sometimes helps one to see an opponent's arguments in a more human way. For example, Sister Helen Prejean, one of the nation's most visible opponents of capital punishment, has been deeply affected by her interactions with the families of murder victims. Seeing the families' grief and pain, she understands much better why people support the death penalty, and she is able to carry out her advocacy with a greater sensitivity to the needs and beliefs of those who do not agree with her. Her relativism, in turn, lends credibility to her work. Dismissing the other side of the argument as totally without merit can be too easy—it is far more useful to understand the nature of the controversy and the reasons *why* the issue defies resolution.

The most controversial issues of all are often those that center on a constitutional right. The Bill of Rights—the first ten amendments to the U.S. Constitution—spells out some of the most fundamental rights that distinguish the governmental system of the United States from those that allow fewer (or other) freedoms. But the sparsely worded document is open to interpretation, and clauses of only a few words are often at the heart of national debates. The Bill of Rights was meant to protect individual liberties; but the needs of some individuals clash with those of society as a whole, and when this happens someone has to decide where to draw the line. Thus the Constitution becomes a battleground between the rights of individuals to do as they please and the responsibility of the government to protect its citizens. The First Amendment's guarantee of "freedom of speech," for example, leads to a number of difficult questions. Some forms of expression, such as burning an American flag, lead to public outrage—but nevertheless are said to be protected by the First Amendment. Other types of expression that most people find objectionable, such as sexually explicit material involving children, are not protected because they are considered harmful. The question is not only where to draw the line, but how to do this without infringing on the personal liberties on which the United States was built.

The Bill of Rights raises many other questions about individual rights and the societal "good." Is a prayer before a high school football game an "establishment of religion" prohibited by the First Amendment? Does the Second Amendment's promise of "the right to bear arms" include concealed handguns? Is stopping and frisking someone standing on a corner known to be frequented by drug dealers a form of "unreasonable search and seizure" in violation of the Fourth Amendment? Although the nine-member U.S. Supreme Court has the ultimate authority in interpreting the Constitution, its answers do not always satisfy the public. When a group of nine people—sometimes by a five-to-four vote—makes a decision that affects the lives of hundreds of millions, public outcry can be expected. And the composition of the Court does change over time, so even a landmark decision is not guaranteed to stand forever. The limits of constitutional protection are always in flux.

These issues make headlines, divide courts, and decide elections. They are the questions most worthy of national debate, and this series aims to cover them as thoroughly as possible. Each volume sets out some of the key arguments surrounding a particular issue, even some views that most people consider extreme or radical—but presents a balanced perspective on the issue. Excerpts from the relevant laws and judicial opinions and references to central concepts, source material, and advocacy groups help the reader to explore the issues even further and to read "the letter of the law" just as the legislatures and the courts have established it.

It may seem that some debates—such as those over capital punishment and abortion, debates with a strong moral component— will never be resolved. But American history offers numerous examples of controversies that once seemed insurmountable but now are effectively settled, even if only on the surface. Abolitionists met with widespread resistance to their efforts to end slavery, and the controversy over that issue threatened to cleave the nation in two; but today public debate over the merits of slavery would be unthinkable, though racial inequalities still plague the nation. Similarly unthinkable at one time was suffrage for women and minorities, but this is now a matter of course. Distributing information about contraception once was a crime. Societies change, and attitudes change, and new questions of social justice are raised constantly while the old ones fade into irrelevancy.

Whatever the root of the controversy, the books in POINT/ COUNTERPOINT seek to explain to the reader the origins of the debate, the current state of the law, and the arguments on both sides. The goal of the series is to inform the reader about the issues facing not only American politicians, but all of the nation's citizens, and to encourage the reader to become more actively involved in resolving these debates, as a voter, a concerned citizen, a journalist, an activist, or an elected official. Democracy is based on education, and every voice counts—so every opinion must be an informed one.

---

This volume asks whether lawsuits have gotten out of control or are necessary to protect the "little person" from irresponsible people and corporations. When a jury awarded nearly $3 million to a grandmother who spilled hot coffee on herself in a McDonald's parking lot, it was a rallying call for supporters of tort reform, or limiting the ability to bring lawsuits for money. However, the story has another side: McDonald's kept its coffee much hotter than other restaurants did, even though a number of customers had reported serious burns. The jury based the amount of its award on the value of two days of coffee sales chain-wide. To some, lawsuits are a legitimate method of protecting people from harm and discouraging misbehavior. Tort reformers, however, argue that lawsuits raise the costs of goods and services, including medical care, and that they primarily benefit the lawyers who file the lawsuits. This volume explores whether such a problem exists, and whether proposed solutions are reasonable.

# Civil Justice and Tort Law

Most Americans have heard of Stella Liebeck's lawsuit against McDonald's Corporation. Liebeck bought a cup of coffee at a McDonald's restaurant and spilled it on her lap, burning herself. She sued McDonald's, and a jury awarded her nearly 3 million dollars in damages. Critics of our civil justice system view Liebeck's lawsuit as the symbol of a "litigation explosion" that punishes innocent businesses. They also contend that litigation hurts the economy. Tillinghast–Towers Perrin, a consulting firm, estimated that, in 2003, lawsuits cost the economy 246 billion dollars—$845 for every man, woman, and child in America. It also found that, since 1975, tort costs have grown by 9.2 percent per year, faster than either the rate of inflation or the rate of economic growth. Defenders reply that the civil justice system, although not perfect, is effective. They accuse reformers of exaggerating the problem of "junk" litigation and maintain that lawsuits benefit society by keeping hazardous products off the market and curbing corporate wrongdoing.

> • **Does our legal system make it too easy for people to avoid responsibility for their actions?**

## Calls for Reform

Beginning in the 1970s, many Americans concluded that the justice system had gone too far in the direction of compensating the injured. The reform movement gained momentum in the 1980s, when pro-business forces gained control of state legislatures— an important battlefield because most civil cases are decided under state law. Proposals for reform included the following:

- Making it easier to weed out baseless lawsuits

- Keeping "junk science" out of the courtroom

- Limiting the amount of money a court can award

- Holding lawyers accountable for abusing the legal system

Reformers' main focus is on tort cases such as medical malpractice, product liability, and personal injury cases. For that reason, proposals to change the system are called "tort reform."

Tort law is part of our common-law tradition. Lawyer and author Philip Howard explained:

> The common law is not a legislative enactment but the synthesis of general standards derived from countless court decisions. We must drive our cars reasonably, for example, or else be accountable to those we injure.
>
> The common law is the opposite of ironclad rules that seek to predetermine results. Application of the common law

always depends on the circumstances. . . . More than anything else, the common law glorifies the particular and invites common sense. It was the common law that developed the jury system, in which a group of peers, not an expert in law, would decide right and wrong in each case. Since it grows with every new court decision, the common law also evolves with changing times.[1]

Over the centuries, courts have reshaped tort law to reflect changes in the way we live.

- **Is the law too hard for the average person to understand? Are lawyers doing enough to make it understandable?**

## FROM THE BENCH

## Public Policy and Liability: *Brown* v. *Kendall* and *Palsgraf* v. *Long Island Railroad Company*

One of the most important developments in tort law was the legal standard of negligence. It grew out of a lawsuit that literally resulted from a dogfight. When his dog started fighting with another, George Kendall used a long stick to separate them. He accidentally hit George Brown, the owner of the other dog, in the eye.

In Brown's suit against Kendall, the trial judge instructed the jury to find Kendall liable unless it found that Kendall had used "extraordinary care" in separating the dogs. He also told them that Brown had the burden of proof. The jury found in Brown's favor, and Kendall appealed.

In *Brown* v. *Kendall*, 60 Mass. 292 (1850), the Supreme Court of Massachusetts reversed the trial court's decision and sent the case back for a new trial. Chief Justice Lemuel Shaw, who wrote the court's opinion, found that Kendall's actions were both lawful and unintentional. That being the case, he concluded that Brown had the burden of proving Kendall was liable. In order to do so, Brown had to show that he acted with ordinary care and Kendall did not.

*Brown* v. *Kendall* is an example of how courts modify the law in response to social changes. At the time, businesses argued that the centuries-old standard of strict liability was not only outdated but bad for the economy. The new, fault-based standard made them less vulnerable to lawsuits. As a result, they were able to keep and reinvest more of their money.

## Civil Versus Criminal Law

Tort law belongs to the civil, as opposed to the criminal, branch of the law. The two trials that involved O.J. Simpson illustrate the difference between them. After the police found evidence that linked Simpson to the murder of his ex-wife, Nicole Brown Simpson, and her friend, Ronald Goldman, the district attorney charged him with the crime of murder. A crime is an offense against society, and the district attorney acts as society's lawyer. Criminal punishment serves a number of purposes: It avenges the crime (we often say that the offender pays his "debt to society"); it deters, or discourages the offender from committing more crimes; and it warns others that they, too, will be punished if they break the law.

One of the most famous negligence cases, *Palsgraf* v. *Long Island Railroad Company*, 248 N.Y. 339, 162 N.E. 99 (1928), also dealt with the issue of when a defendant should be held responsible for injuring another. This case began when two railroad employees helped a man board a train. In doing so, they dislodged a package of fireworks the man was carrying. The fireworks exploded and the shock knocked down some scales "many feet away," injuring Helen Palsgraf.

Palsgraf sued the railroad for negligence. The lower courts ruled in her favor, but New York's highest court ruled by a 4–3 vote that the railroad was not liable. Chief Judge Benjamin Cardozo wrote the majority opinion. In his view, the issue was not simply whether the railroad's employees were negligent—there was no question that they were—but also whether they were liable to Palsgraf. Underlying his analysis was the recognition that it would not be fair to hold a defendant liable for remote consequences of his negligence. Cardozo concluded that Palsgraf was outside the "zone of danger" because the railroad's employees could not have foreseen her being injured: "If no hazard was apparent to the eye of ordinary vigilance, an act innocent and harmless, at least to outward seeming, *with reference to her*, did not take to itself the quality of a tort because it happened to be a wrong . . . with reference to some one else" (emphasis added).

Because of the serious consequences involved, the U.S. Constitution provides the defendant, the person charged with a crime, with a number of legal safeguards against being unfairly convicted. These include the rights to be represented by a lawyer, to be tried by a jury, and to remain silent. In addition, the prosecutor must prove guilt beyond a reasonable doubt.

In O.J. Simpson's criminal trial, the prosecution argued that blood stains found at the crime scene matched those at Simpson's house. The evidence strongly suggested that Simpson was the killer, but his lawyers maintained that the police had tampered with it. They succeeded in raising enough doubt about the evidence that the jury found Simpson not guilty. That verdict did not end Simpson's legal problems. The victims' families filed a civil lawsuit against Simpson, alleging that he had wrongfully caused Brown Simpson's and Goldman's deaths.

There are important differences between a civil suit and a criminal suit. A civil suit is brought by the victim, not a government official, and the victim can sue even if criminal charges are never filed. The objective of a civil suit is not to punish the wrongdoer but to recover a sum of money, called damages. The court ordered Simpson to pay his victims' families 33.5 million dollars. A civil defendant enjoys less constitutional protection than a criminal defendant does, and the plaintiff needs to prove his or her case by only a preponderance, or majority, of the evidence.

> • **Have "celebrity trials" made Americans more knowledgeable about the legal system? Or have these trials made them more cynical?**

## What Is a Tort?

*Black's Law Dictionary* defines the term *tort* as "a civil wrong, other than breach of contract, for which a remedy may be obtained, usually in the form of damages . . . a breach of the duty that the law imposes on persons who stand in a particular

**Although O.J. Simpson was not convicted in a criminal trial, he was forced to pay damages to Nicole Brown Simpson's and Ron Goldman's families when he lost the civil trial. Here, Goldman's family arrives at Los Angeles County Superior Court in Santa Monica, California, after the jury awarded them 12.5 million dollars in the punitive phase of the civil trial.**

relation to one another."[2] Tort law imposes rules of behavior, often called "duties," that are based on community standards of how people should act. The other branch of civil law, the law of contracts, imposes duties based on a voluntary agreement between people.

Tort law originated in medieval England, when courts recognized a person's right to sue someone who injured him. Since then, the right to sue has been extended to a variety of other injuries. Tort cases were rare until the Industrial Revolution, when the widespread use of machinery increased the chance that innocent people would be harmed. That presented courts with a problem: If they applied existing legal principles and ruled in favor of victims, businesses could be bankrupted and the economy might suffer. As a result, they adopted a new legal standard of negligence: The injured person had to prove that the person who injured him was at fault. The negligence standard favored businesses and sometimes led to harsh results.

As tort cases multiplied in the late nineteenth century, legal scholars found it necessary to organize this quickly growing field of law. They divided torts into three categories, which are recognized today. The first consists of intentional torts, many of which are analogous to criminal acts. The second category of torts is negligence. The law of negligence requires people to act with ordinary care—in other words, "that kind and degree of care, which prudent and cautious men would use, such as is required by the exigency of the case, and such as is necessary to guard against probable danger."[3] When a person's conduct falls below that standard and causes harm to another, he or she can be found liable. One area of negligence is medical malpractice. The law requires a doctor to have "that reasonable degree of learning and skill that is ordinarily possessed by physicians and surgeons in the locality where he practices."[4]

The third category of torts involves strict liability. In some circumstances, a person can be held liable for injuring another person even if he or she exercised ordinary care. Originally, courts limited the strict-liability standard to those who engaged in "ultrahazardous activities" such as using dynamite. Starting in the 1960s, courts extended it to consumer products. In *Greenman v. Yuba Power Products*, 59 Cal. 2d 57, 377 P.2d 897 (1963), the Supreme Court of California held that "a manufacturer is strictly liable in tort when an article he places on the market, knowing that it is to be used without inspection for defects, proves to have a defect that causes injury to a human being."[5]

- **Does strict liability lead to safer products?**

A plaintiff must not only prove wrongdoing on the part of the defendant but also overcome any legal defenses that would excuse the defendant from liability. One defense is lack of causation: The link between the defendant's action and the plaintiff's injuries was too remote for the law to recognize a right to recover. Another defense is the plaintiff's own behavior. Under today's standard of comparative negligence, the jury must allocate fault among the parties. In most states, a plaintiff who is partially at fault can still recover, but the recovery will be reduced by the plaintiff's percentage of fault. Other defenses based on the plaintiff's conduct include assumption of the risk, for example, when a baseball fan sits in the front row behind the dugout even though he knew that a baseball could hit him if he sat there, and misuse or alteration of the product that caused the injury. Some defenses are based on notions of fairness, such as statutes of repose, which provide that a manufacturer is not liable for injuries that occurred more than a given number of years after a product was sold.

## Damages

It has been said that "the law cannot undo the physical consequences of an injury. What it does instead is award money damages in an attempt to compensate the injured plaintiff for the loss suffered at the hands of the defendant."[6] Damages are often classified as economic and noneconomic. Economic damages include a broken window, doctor and hospital bills, and wages lost because of injuries. Calculating the amount of these damages is relatively straightforward. Noneconomic damages are harder to measure. They include injury to reputation, physical pain associated with an injury, and humiliation,

*(continued on page 20)*

# FROM THE BENCH

# Strict-Tort Liability:
## *Greenman* v. *Yuba Power Products, Inc.*

Fifty years ago, a consumer injured by a defective product could sue under one of two legal theories. One was negligence, a lack of ordinary care in designing or manufacturing the project. The other was breach of warranty, an agreement between the seller and consumer that a product would meet certain standards. An express warranty is created by specific statements about the product; an implied warranty is a requirement, imposed by law, that the product is fit for its intended use.

Many legal scholars criticized those legal theories because they made it too difficult for consumers to recover. In *Greenman* v. *Yuba Power Products,* 59 Cal. 2d 57, 377 P.2d 897 (1963), the Supreme Court of California agreed with them. It applied a different legal theory, strict-tort liability, to product-liability cases.

The case began when William Greenman was seriously injured while using a Shopsmith, a power tool manufactured by Yuba Power Products. Greenman sued Yuba Power and the store that sold his wife the Shopsmith. His complaint alleged both negligence and breach of warranty.

A Superior Court jury ordered Yuba Power to pay Greenman $65,000. It found that Yuba Power was negligent in designing and manufacturing the Shopsmith and that language in the Shopsmith brochure, which described it as "rugged" and having "positive locks that hold adjustments," created a warranty. Yuba Power appealed, arguing that Greenman failed to it give the legally required notice of breach of warranty.

The case reached the Supreme Court of California, which unanimously affirmed the Superior Court's decision. Justice Roger Traynor wrote the court's opinion. Although he agreed that Yuba Power was liable, Justice Traynor based his decision on strict-tort liability. He observed that it was not a new legal theory but rather the adaptation of existing strict-liability standards to product-liability cases. He added that requiring a consumer to notify the manufacturer was "not ... appropriate ... in actions by injured consumers against manufacturers with whom they have not dealt." He went on to state:

> As between the immediate parties to the sale [the notice requirement] is a sound commercial rule, designed to protect the seller against unduly delayed claims for damages. As applied to personal injuries, and notice to a remote seller, it becomes a booby-trap for the unwary. The injured consumer is seldom steeped in the business practice which justifies the rule ... and at least until he has had legal advice it will not occur to him to give notice to one with whom he has had no dealings.

Although some experts criticized *Greenman* as an example of judicial activism, courts in other states followed its reasoning. In 1965, the American Law Institute, an influential organization of legal scholars, incorporated strict-tort liability into the *Restatement (Second) of Torts*, a compilation of the basic principles of tort law. Section 402A of the *Restatement* provided:

(1) One who sells any product in a defective condition unreasonably dangerous to the user or consumer or to his property is subject to liability for physical harm thereby caused to the ultimate user or consumer, or to his property, if

   (a) the seller is engaged in the business of selling such a product, and

   (b) it is expected to and does reach the user or consumer without substantial change in the condition in which it is sold.

(2) The rule stated in Subsection (1) applies although

   (a) the seller has exercised all possible care in the preparation and sale of his product, and

   (b) the user or consumer has not bought the product from or entered into any contractual relation with the seller.

Since 1965, both product liability law and §402A have been expanded and interpreted by thousands of court decisions. The *Restatement (Third) of Torts*, published in 1998, sets out standards of strict-tort liability.

Strict-tort liability makes it unnecessary for a person injured by a defective product to prove careless design or bad workmanship by the manufacturer. Instead, he or she can win the case by proving one of the following:

- The product failed to meet consumer expectations (for example, the consumer drove a Ford Bronco equipped with Firestone tires, which was at greater risk of rolling over if the tire tread separated).

- The product's risks outweigh its benefits (for example, the lawnmower that injured the consumer was more dangerous than other brands on the market).

- The manufacturer failed to warn about the risks of using the product (for example, the consumer took a prescription drug with side effects he or she was unaware of).

*(continued from page 17)*

among others. Although an award of damages cannot compensate for losses such as the death of a loved one, the money provides some comfort and holds the defendant responsible for his or her wrongdoing. Both economic and noneconomic damages are compensatory, or intended to make up for injuries suffered.

In cases of flagrant wrongdoing, courts have the authority to award punitive damages. This concept was first recognized by an English court in a 1763 case, *Wilkes* v. *Wood*,[7] which involved the unlawful search of a home. In that case, the judge not only reaffirmed the principle that it was up to the jury to decide how much to award but also told the jurors that they were free "to give damages for more than the injury received." It has been said that punitive damages "reduce the defendant's incentive to engage in wrongful conduct, acting as a big stick that requires a potential wrongdoer to think twice about the consequences of his or her actions."[8] When assessing punitive damages, the jury is allowed to consider how much money the defendant has. Stella Liebeck's lawyer told the jury that McDonald's sold 1.35 million dollars' worth of coffee per day. The jury decided that two days' worth of revenue from coffee sales was an appropriate punishment for the company's disregard for its customers' safety.

> • **Do punitive damages discourage corporate wrongdoing or are they a windfall for plaintiffs and their lawyers?**

## Summary

Many Americans believe that our system of civil justice makes it too easy to sue and that lawsuits unfairly penalize innocent businesses. Most civil suits arise under tort law, a set of common-law principles under which an injured person can recover damages from the party whose wrongdoing injured him or her.

Tort law covers a broad range of conduct that harms others, including intentional conduct and failing to act with ordinary care toward others. Sometimes, for reasons of fairness, the law imposes strict liability, requiring a person to pay those whom he or she injured even though he or she was not at fault. Today, some of the most controversial tort cases are those that allege that a product is defective or that a doctor committed malpractice.

# The Steps in a Civil Case

The Introduction dealt primarily with substantive law, which defines rights and responsibilities. This chapter focuses on procedural law, which can be analogized to the rules of a game. Rules of procedure promote the orderly decision of lawsuits and, more important, make sure that parties are treated fairly in court. Fairness is critical because the Constitution's due process clause forbids a state to "deprive any person of life, liberty, or property, without due process of law."[9] The distinction between procedural and substantive law is not always clear. Sometimes, a question of procedure decides the outcome of a lawsuit.

> • Is it more important to follow legal procedures or to make sure that justice is served, even if procedures aren't followed?

## Starting the Lawsuit

Millions of Americans suffer injuries, but only a small fraction of them sues as a result. Lawyer and author Jay Feinman described the findings of one massive study of civil litigation:

> First take a roundup of, say, 10,000 bad experiences of all kinds—a slip on a neighbor's icy sidewalk, a new toaster that burns the bread, a landlord's failure to provide enough hot water to a tenant. The injured party in 1,000 of these incidents will see herself as the victim of a wrong caused by some other person (the neighbor, the manufacturer of the toaster, the landlord). Of these people, 700 will complain to the wrongdoer about the problem; the other 300 will let it go. The wrongdoer will reject the claim in 450 of the cases, and the victim will go see a lawyer in about 100 of those cases. The lawyer will file a case in court in 50 cases.[10]

Because many people with valid legal claims have little money, plaintiffs' lawyers created the contingent-fee arrangement. As lawyer-authors Ralph Nader and Wesley Smith explain, "A lawyer agrees to take a case without any money up front and without requiring the client to pay an hourly or flat fee. In return, the lawyer is entitled to receive a percentage of the actual amount of money collected, generally 33 percent, but sometimes 40 percent if the case has gone through trial and/or appeal."[11]

Once the lawyer takes the case, he or she must decide whom to sue. If the person primarily at fault has no money, it makes no sense to sue unless there is another defendant who was also at fault and does have money. In lawyers' language, those defendants have "deep pockets." Deep-pockets defendants are often only slightly at fault, however.

Another critical question is where to file suit. Sometimes the lawyer can choose from among several states. If the lawyer represents a driver who was injured in an out-of-state traffic crash, he or she can sue where the crash occurred, where the other driver lives, or in the client's home state. Each state has different rules of substantive law, which determine how much the plaintiff can recover and even whether he or she has a valid claim in the first place. If there is a choice of states, the lawyer will file in the state that seems most favorable.

Traditionally, a lawsuit pitted one plaintiff against one defendant. Today, however, many cases involve multiple parties. Some involve numerous plaintiffs, all of whom allege that they were victims of the same wrongdoing by the same defendant. To avoid the time and expense of repeatedly litigating the same facts, courts permit class-action suits, in which a small number of plaintiffs appear in court on behalf of the entire class.

The plaintiff starts the lawsuit by filing a complaint with the court. The complaint is a document that alleges what the defendant did and how much money the plaintiff is asking for. The lawyer must also send the defendant a copy of the complaint so that he or she has notice of the lawsuit and a chance to mount a defense in court.

## Challenging the Lawsuit

Once the defendant has been notified, he or she has several options. One is to ask to have the suit dismissed, or thrown out of court. This is done by filing a motion, or formal request, to the judge to explain why dismissal is appropriate. Out-of-state defendants often move to dismiss on the grounds of lack of jurisdiction, or legal authority over them. The U.S. Supreme Court has held that "a state court may exercise personal jurisdiction over a nonresident defendant only so long as there exist 'minimum contacts' between the defendant and the forum State." [12] Another argument for dismissal is that the statute of limitations has run out. This law requires a plaintiff to file suit within a given time after being injured or else lose the right to sue.

Still another reason for dismissal is failure to state a cause of action—that is, a set of facts that entitles the plaintiff to a legal remedy. A cause of action consists of a number of elements, for example, that a product was unreasonably dangerous and the plaintiff suffered injuries while using it. The plaintiff must allege all of those elements in the complaint. He or she eventually has to prove them but does not need to do so at this stage. Some cases are dismissed because the plaintiff has raised a new legal theory that the court refuses to accept. A few are dismissed because they are frivolous, in other words, the party's "primary purpose . . . was to harass, embarrass, or injure" the other party; the party "had no reasonable basis to believe the facts underlying [his] legal position were in fact true," or "the party's legal position was devoid of arguable legal merit."[13]

> • **Are courts biased against corporations? Against out-of-state defendants?**

If the defendant cannot get the case dismissed, he or she must challenge it on the merits. Typically, the defendant files an answer, a document that disputes the plaintiff's version of the facts and challenges the plaintiff to come forward with evidence to prove the claim. The complaint, the answer, and other documents filed by the parties are called "pleadings." They define the issues to be decided in the case.

## Discovery

Once the issues are defined, the focus of the case shifts to gathering evidence. The rules that govern this stage today are different from those of the past. Our legal system relies heavily on the adversary system, under which "counsel for each side determines what evidence will be brought forward, by which witnesses, in what order, and which issues will emerge and with what kind of emphasis."[14]

Traditionally, the judge's role was like that of an umpire in a baseball game. He or she ruled when asked to but otherwise did not intervene. During the 1930s, the Supreme Court adopted the Federal Rules of Civil Procedure, and most states adopted similar rules. These rules were designed in part to "make a trial less a game of blindman's buff and more a fair contest with the basic issues and facts disclosed to the fullest practicable extent."[15] The most dramatic changes involved discovery, or the exchange of evidence before trial. The rules of discovery require a party to turn over the relevant evidence it

## FROM THE BENCH

### The Importance of Jurisdiction:
### *World-Wide Volkswagen Corporation* v. *Woodson*

During the twentieth century, the U.S. Supreme Court ruled that it was constitutional for states to exercise "long-arm" jurisdiction over out-of-state defendants, especially corporations. The case of *World-Wide Volkswagen Corporation* v. *Woodson*, 444 U.S. 286 (1980), dealt with the limits of such jurisdiction.

The case began when the Robinsons, who were from New York, were involved in a traffic crash in Oklahoma. Another driver rear-ended their car, and the resulting fire seriously burned Kay Robinson and her two children. The other driver was at fault. Many at-fault drivers lack the money and insurance coverage to pay for serious injuries, and that appeared to be the case in this situation. As a result, the Robinsons looked for other defendants. Alleging that their vehicle was defective, they sued the German manufacturer and American importer of their car in state court in Oklahoma. They also sued World-Wide Volkswagen Corporation, the Audi distributor for the New York area, and Seaway Volkswagen, the dealer.

World-Wide and Seaway asked the trial judge, Charles Woodson, to dismiss them from the case. They argued that, because their businesses were limited to the New York area, forcing them to defend a lawsuit in Oklahoma would deny them due process of law. After Judge Woodson denied their motion, they appealed to the Supreme Court of Oklahoma, which upheld the decision.

World-Wide and Seaway appealed to the U.S. Supreme Court which ruled by a 6–3 vote that Oklahoma's courts lacked jurisdiction over them. Justice Byron White wrote the majority opinion. Even though the national economy had become more interdependent, Justice White concluded that due process still required "minimum contacts" between an out-of-state defendant and the state where it was sued. The minimum-contacts requirement had two functions: It possesses, even if it helps the other party's case. If necessary, the judge will order a party to turn over evidence or else face serious consequences. According to Ralph Nader and Wesley Smith, "Discovery can facilitate settlements and eliminate disruptive and unfair surprises at trial. The more at stake in the case, usually the more pretrial workup

protected a defendant against having to respond to a case in a faraway court, and it kept state courts from encroaching on the jurisdiction of other states. In this case, neither World-Wide nor Seaway had the required minimum contacts with Oklahoma because they had no physical presence in that state and had not done business there. Justice White rejected Oklahoma's arguments for exercising jurisdiction. Although World-Wide and Seaway might have foreseen that a customer would drive a car in Oklahoma, they did not put their cars into the stream of commerce expecting Oklahomans to buy them. Also, although they earned some revenue as a result of their cars being driven in Oklahoma, that was too remote a contact to subject them to the state's jurisdiction.

Justices William Brennan, Thurgood Marshall, and Harry Blackmun dissented. They offered several reasons why it would be fair to let Oklahoma take jurisdiction over World-Wide and Seaway. They argued that, in a modern national economy, the minimum-contacts standard was too protective of defendants selling products—especially cars—capable of being used in other states. In addition, they argued that Oklahoma had an interest in deciding the Robinsons' lawsuit because they had been injured there, many potential witnesses were located in that state, and World-Wide and Seaway derived benefits from Oklahoma, including that state's investment in its highway system.

Sometimes, who the parties are determines where a case will be tried. Under federal law, a party in a civil case has the right to remove the case to federal court if there is diversity of citizenship, meaning that the parties are citizens of different states. Parties, especially defendants, remove cases when they believe that state courts will not treat them fairly. Some state courts have a reputation for favoring plaintiffs, and trial lawyers would rather try the case there than in federal court.

performed. It isn't glamourous and it isn't fun, but it is where most lawsuits are made or broken."[16] The new rules also gave judges more control over lawsuits, including the authority to weed out weak cases before they reach the jury and to encourage the parties to reach a settlement.

• **What is your opinion of the legal profession? What would you do to improve its image?**

## Trial

More than 95 percent of lawsuits are settled before trial. Trials occur only when the two sides have serious differences over how much the case is worth or when one side wants to establish a legal precedent that will affect other cases. The parties sometimes agree to try their case before a judge, but they usually ask for a jury trial. In federal cases, the Constitution provides, "In Suits at common law, where the value in controversy shall exceed twenty dollars, the right of trial by jury shall be preserved."[17] Most state constitutions similarly provide for jury trial in civil cases. Philip Howard observed, "The jury system does not produce results like a scientific theorem; it is more akin to a roll of the dice. But a jury is impartial, and it can weigh all the circumstances. That's the best we can do."[18]

Jurors are laypersons, "amateurs" who know little about the law and nothing about the facts of the case other than what they hear in court. At the trial, the parties tell them a story, using live witnesses and physical evidence such as DNA analysis. Each party challenges the other's story by objecting to evidence that it considers inappropriate and by questioning the other side's witnesses to expose bias or faulty recollections. Strict rules of evidence govern the trial. Lawyers may present only relevant evidence and may not appeal to the jurors' emotions or prejudice.

• **If you were a defendant in a civil case, would you trust a jury to decide your fate?**

Some evidence takes the form of expert testimony. On occasion, jurors need help from someone with specialized knowledge. That is especially true in malpractice cases. In the film *The Verdict*, a young woman suffered brain damage after her doctor administered a general anesthetic too soon after she ate. In that case, the jurors could not determine, on the basis of their own knowledge and experience, whether the woman had been injured as the result of her doctor's negligence. Her lawyer had to call an expert to the stand to explain what were the proper medical procedures under those circumstances.

## Judgment and Appeal

The jury is responsible for deciding questions of fact; what inferences to draw from the evidence, such as skid marks at a crash scene; and whether witnesses are believable. It also determines who should win and, if the plaintiff should, how much money he or she should be awarded. That determination is called the "verdict." It is up to the judge to decide legal issues, such as whether testimony should be admitted. The judge has a great deal of latitude to modify the jury's verdict or even overrule it. The decision as to who won and how much the plaintiff should recover is called the "judgment."

> • **Are juries capable of deciding cases that involve science and medicine? Should complex cases be tried by a judge with no jury?**

The losing party can appeal the judgment to a higher court. An appeal will succeed only if the lower court made a legal error serious enough to affect the outcome of the case. The purpose of appeals court decisions is to make sure that lower courts apply the law correctly and to make the law more uniform. For that reason, the decisions are in writing, and most are published in book form and on the Internet. Judges and lawyers rely on the legal principles set out in those decisions.

## Summary

The rules of civil procedure promote the orderly handling of cases and ensure that a party is given due process of law. The plaintiff starts the lawsuit and has the burden of proof. The defendant has several opportunities to defeat the lawsuit:

## FROM THE BENCH

## Limiting Punitive Damages: *State Farm Mutual Automobile Insurance Company* v. *Campbell*

Curtis Campbell was sued after a fatal traffic crash. His insurer, State Farm Mutual Insurance Company, turned down an offer to settle for $50,000 and insisted on trying the case. The court found Campbell liable and entered judgment against him for nearly $185,000. State Farm refused to pay until a year and a half later.

Campbell and his wife sued State Farm, alleging bad faith, fraud, and intentional infliction of emotional distress. At the trial, they presented evidence that State Farm's delay in paying was part of a nationwide strategy of bad-faith handling of claims. A District Court jury awarded the Campbells 2.6 million dollars in compensatory damages and 145 million dollars in punitive damages. The judge reduced the punitive-damage award to 25 million dollars, but the Supreme Court of Utah reinstated the original amount. In doing so, it cited State Farm's reprehensible conduct and great wealth and the fact that it had mistreated 50,000 policyholders and had not been punished for it.

State Farm appealed to the U.S. Supreme Court, arguing that the Utah courts had denied it due process of law. It relied on an earlier Court decision, *BMW of North America* v. *Gore*, 517 U.S. 559 (1996), which held that a "grossly excessive" punitive-damage award was a denial of due process. *Gore* set out guidelines, but no clear standard, for determining whether an award was grossly excessive.

In *State Farm Mutual Automobile Insurance Company* v. *Campbell*, 538 U.S. 408 (2003), the Supreme Court agreed with State Farm. In a 6–3 vote to reverse the judgment, it sent the case back to the Utah courts to reassess punitive damages, with the strong suggestion that an award larger than one million dollars would be unconstitutional.

Moving to dismiss it, moving for judgment before or after trial, rebutting the plaintiff's case at trial, or appealing to a higher court. Because juries are made of laypersons, strict rules apply to the presentation of evidence, especially expert testimony. Juries decide issues of fact and decide who should prevail. The judge has considerable control over the case, however, including the power to modify or even overrule the jury's decision.

Justice Anthony Kennedy wrote the majority opinion. Applying the *Gore* criteria, he concluded that a punitive-damage award 145 times the compensatory-damage award was excessive. He first found that, although State Farm's actions were "reprehensible," the Utah courts had punished the company for conduct that occurred outside the state and that did not directly affect the Campbells. He warned that such an approach could result in multiple awards of punitive damages for the same conduct. He next concluded that, as a general rule, punitive-damage awards more than four times compensatory damages were excessive. That rule was not hard and fast, however. A higher ratio might be appropriate in cases where compensatory damages were small, and vice versa. In this case, the District Court had awarded the Campbells a substantial amount of compensatory damages, especially considering that the harm to them was mental, not physical or economic. Finally, he found that the punitive-damages award was far greater than the most relevant financial penalty under Utah law—a $10,000 fine for fraud.

Justices Antonin Scalia and Clarence Thomas dissented. They argued, as they did in *Gore*, that the due process clause did not limit state courts' power to award punitive damages.

Justice Ruth Bader Ginsberg also dissented. She agreed with Justices Scalia and Thomas that it was up to the states to limit punitive damages. She also maintained that State Farm's wrongdoing justified a 145-million-dollar award. The record, she noted, revealed that top management directed employees to pressure claimants—especially vulnerable ones—to accept inadequate settlements, lie about policyholders to reduce the value of their claims, pad files with self-serving documents and leave critical items out of files, and destroy evidence of company wrongdoing.

# America Is Experiencing a "Litigation Explosion"

**F**ifty years ago, the law tended to favor defendants. Since then, courts and legislatures have attempted to put plaintiffs on a more equal footing. Tort reformers argue that those changes have stirred up litigation. Lawyer and author Walter Olson explained:

> The older law was by no means immune to the problem of meritless suits, but it did go to some lengths to discourage them. Pleadings focused immediate attention on the merits of a case. Objective triggers and no-guesswork rules of evidence and damages gave both sides a better idea of which cases belonged in court and which did not. Procedural rules tried to keep in check the cost impositions litigants could inflict on each other.[19]

Reformers believe that it is time to roll back recent changes to the law and once again make lawsuits a last resort.

## There are too many lawsuits.

According to the National Center for State Courts (NCSC), civil cases increased by 38 percent between 1975 and 2001, despite no-fault auto insurance and other measures aimed at reducing the number of suits that involved traffic crashes. Medical malpractice claims increased by 24 percent between 1992 and 2001. A total of 16 million civil suits were filed in 2002, the highest ever, and tort cases account for a substantial percentage of that total.

One reason why there are so many lawsuits is that there are so many lawyers to file them. In 2004, there was 1 lawyer for every 270 Americans; in 1951, there was 1 for every 695 people. At the same time, traditional restrictions on the legal profession have been loosened. For years, the rules of ethics barred lawyers from publicizing themselves. Those who did so could be disbarred—that is, expelled from the profession. In *Bates* v. *State Bar of Arizona*, 433 U.S. 570 (1975), the Supreme Court ruled that lawyers had a First Amendment right to advertise their services. *Bates* and later court decisions legalized many forms of advertising and even allowed lawyers to directly solicit clients—a practice some critics call "ambulance chasing." Critics argue that the new rules have created a class of "entrepreneurial" lawyers: "That is the lawyer who engineers a case from the very inception; the lawyer who finds 'clients' to serve as parties to the benefit primarily of the lawyer and to the possible detriment of the civil justice system."[20] The legal profession has also been accused of a "win at all costs" mentality: Aggressive behavior, once frowned on, has become the norm. Furthermore, some plaintiffs "shop" for a lawyer willing to take a weak case.

> • **Does America have too many lawyers? Should talented people be encouraged to go into other fields, such as teaching?**

## Litigation has become too costly.

The Tillinghast–Towers Perrin consulting firm estimates that the costs of tort litigation add up to 2.2 percent of the nation's gross domestic product (GDP), which is the value of all goods and services produced by a country in a given period of time,[21] a much higher percentage than other Western countries. Reformers argue that tort costs inhibit economic growth because they have the same effect as a tax: "A car, a power tool, and a ladder cost more because manufacturers are forced to include unnecessary safety devices or warnings. Physicians must practice defensive medicine . . . or they leave high-risk specialties such as obstetrics altogether."[22] They maintain that an American family of four

## Trial Lawyers, Inc.: Litigation Becomes Big Business

Trial lawyers like to portray themselves as champions of ordinary Americans, but their critics charge that a group of wealthy and powerful lawyers have turned the representation of plaintiffs into a business. The Manhattan Institute, a New York "think tank" that supports tort reform, calls plaintiffs' lawyers "Trial Lawyers, Inc."

The institute likens the nation's trial lawyers to a large corporation. Their annual revenues are estimated at nearly 40 billion dollars per year, twice those of the Cola-Cola Company. It is allegedly dominated by "tort kingpins" who specialize in specific types of litigation and who agree to stay out of one another's markets—a practice that is illegal in most other industries. Trial Lawyers, Inc., runs an aggressive and cooperative marketing program, promoting its services on a variety of media, including the Internet.

Like other businesses, Trial Lawyers, Inc., has traditional "profit centers," including asbestos and tobacco litigation and lawsuits against drug makers and insurance companies. Other sources of profit include class-action cases on behalf of consumers and malpractice suits against doctors and hospitals. These cases earn trial lawyers huge fees, most notably the billions they earned representing the states in the tobacco litigation.

Trial Lawyers, Inc., reinvested much of its profit in "potential growth markets," including lawsuits against the makers of lead paint and builders and renters of homes allegedly infected with toxic mold. Some lawyers predict that mold cases will prove as lucrative as asbestos litigation.

pays a "tort tax" of more than $3,300 per year and add that most of that tax goes to lawyers, not victims.

Lawsuits have hit the nation's doctors especially hard. Since 1975, malpractice-related costs have grown by nearly 12 percent per year, considerably faster than tort costs in general. Malpractice accounts for only 5 percent of tort cases, but that still translates into tens of thousands of such cases per year. According to the American Medical Association (AMA), the median jury award in malpractice cases rose by 110 percent between 1994 and 2002 and now stands at more than one million dollars. Even when a doctor wins, the legal costs are considerable. The average cost of defense is $16,000 for suits that are dismissed before the trial starts and

Trial Lawyers, Inc., has become wealthy enough to play the role of venture capitalist, funding speculative lawsuits that might some day generate huge legal fees. One example is suits that allege that fast-food companies deceived customers about the fat and calories in their products. Although these suits have been thrown out of court, trial lawyers point out that suits against tobacco companies also were unsuccessful for years.

According to the institute, tobacco litigation represents another trend: Trial lawyers are acting as an unelected "fourth branch" of government, using the courts to impose regulations opposed by the public or rejected by regulatory agencies. Their lawsuits have targeted not only cigarettes but also guns. They have also sued makers of prescription drugs and birth-control devices, products approved by the FDA. Such litigation allows courts to second-guess the judgment of scientific and medical experts and sometimes even drives legal products off the market.

Finally, the institute accuses Trial Lawyers, Inc., of acting like other special interests by spending heavily to influence the political process. Trial lawyers have given to candidates for the U.S. Senate and House as well as candidates for judgeships—including judges who preside over pro-plaintiff courts.

Source: The Manhattan Institute, *Trial Lawyers, Inc.: A Report on the Lawsuit Industry in America 2003*. New York: The Manhattan Institute, Center for Legal Policy, 2003. Available at *http://www.manhattan-institute.org/triallawyersinc.pdf*.

$92,000 for cases that go to a jury. As a result, doctors have been forced to practice "defensive medicine"—that is, ordering additional treatments, tests, and procedures for the purpose of protecting themselves from lawsuits rather than for diagnosing or treating the patient. According to some estimates, defensive medicine wastes 70 billion to 120 billion dollars per year.

Tort reformers blame litigation for a malpractice insurance crisis. Consider the example of Thomas Selznick, a Detroit-area doctor. Even though he won all 23 malpractice suits against his seven-doctor practice, his insurance company canceled his coverage. According to Selznick, "Because they've had to pay legal fees to defend us, they decided they didn't want to cover us anymore."[23] Even doctors who kept their insurance have been forced to make difficult decisions, as President Bush recently explained:

> For some physicians, even raising costs for patients isn't enough to afford the premium increases caused by these lawsuits. And so, physicians are faced with a terrible choice: Give up medicine entirely, or to move to another place where they can afford to practice medicine. And that problem affects all doctors from family practitioners in rural towns to surgeons in big city hospitals.[24]

The president added that doctors in certain specialties, especially obstetrics and gynecology, were at especially high risk for being sued. As a result, some pregnant women, especially those who live in rural areas, have trouble finding a doctor willing to deliver their babies.

> • **Is there a difference between the legal profession and other businesses? Was it a mistake to let lawyers advertise?**

## The law encourages litigation.
Reformers believe that the abandonment of clear legal rules has

encouraged litigation. For example, courts have found drugs approved by the federal Food and Drug Administration (FDA) to be unreasonably dangerous and have applied novel legal theories to hold tobacco companies liable for marketing a legal product that most Americans knew was unhealthy. Lawmakers share some of the blame as well. The federal Racketeer Influenced and Corrupt Organizations (RICO) Act and many state consumer-protection laws are so broadly worded that it is difficult to dismiss even weak lawsuits. Other laws provide an economic incentive to sue. Section 349 of the New York General Business Law, that state's deceptive-practices law, authorizes triple damages of up to $3,000, plus the plaintiff's legal fees, "if the court finds the defendant willfully or knowingly violated this section."[25] Reformers complain that these laws provide for "one-way" fee awards: A plaintiff who wins can recover his or her lawyer's fees from the other party, but a defendant who wins cannot.

Liberal rules of procedure have made it easier to file class-action suits in which a small number of "named plaintiffs" represent the interests of a larger class of individuals who suffered similar injuries as the result of the same wrongdoing. In theory, class actions serve the public interest by making corporations more accountable, Jay Feinman explains:

> An airline passenger may pay a few dollars more for a plane ticket because the airlines illegally inflated the price of tickets, or a credit card holder may pay a few cents more when a bank miscalculates the interest rate. Because of the small size of the claims and the expense of litigation, it isn't worthwhile for any one of these consumers to sue the airlines or the bank. The collective loss of all passengers or all credit card users, though, is quite large.[26]

Reformers claim that trial lawyers have abused the rules that govern these suits, for example, by recruiting their friends and relatives to serve as named plaintiffs. They also blame judges for allowing cases to go forward as class actions even when the plaintiffs do not have similar claims against the defendant. The result has been nationwide class actions that involve thousands of class members, many of whom have never set foot in the state where the case is being heard. The majority of class members never see their lawyer and have no way of knowing

## THE LETTER OF THE LAW

## The Class Action Fairness Act of 2005

On February 18, 2005, President Bush signed the Class Action Fairness Act of 2005 (Public Law 109-2) into law.

Section 2 of the Act explains why class-action reform is necessary:

- Over the past decade, class-action abuses have harmed plaintiffs with legitimate claims, as well as defendants who had acted responsibly; adversely affected interstate commerce; and undermined public respect for the judicial system.

- Class members have received little benefit from class-action suits and have sometimes even been harmed when courts awarded trial lawyers large fees, whereas class members received near-worthless coupons; when settlements gave some members larger awards than the rest of the class; and when confusing legal notices prevented class members from understanding their rights.

- Allowing state court judges to decide class actions has kept cases of national importance out of federal court, resulted in biased decisions against out-of-state defendants, and allowed one state's courts to impose its view of the law on other states.

To address those problems, the act added the following provisions to Title 28 of the United States Code:

- Section 1332(d) allows federal courts to take jurisdiction over a class-action suit if (a) there are 100 or more plaintiffs, (b) at least one-third of the plaintiffs live outside the state where the suit was filed, and (c) the plaintiffs are demanding a total of more than 5 million dollars.

whether the lawyer or the named plaintiffs are acting in their best interests.

Reformers also argue that personal-injury suits have taken on many aspects of class actions. In particular, they point to mass-tort litigation, which often involves huge numbers of plaintiffs. In the litigation against the makers of Agent Orange, a chemical used to kill vegetation during the Vietnam War, the class grew to

- Section 1453 allows a defendant to move a class-action suit from state court to federal court and provides for a speedy decision of the question of whether the suit should be decided in federal court.

- Section 1712 imposes the following restrictions on settlements in which coupons, rather than cash, are distributed to class members:

  — The judge may not approve a coupon settlement unless he finds that it is "fair, reasonable, and adequate for class members."

  — Legal fees for plaintiffs' lawyers are limited to either a percentage of the value of coupons actually redeemed or an hourly rate based on time spent on the case.

  — The judge can require the defendant to donate to charity part of the value of unreedemed coupons.

- Section 1713 bans settlements under which class members would suffer a net financial loss unless the judge finds that there are noncash benefits that would "substantially outweigh" that loss.

- Section 1714 bans settlements that would pay more money to plaintiffs merely because they live near the court where the suit was filed.

The act also directs the Judicial Conference of the United States to make recommendations concerning "best practices" courts should use to make sure that class-action settlements are fair, and to deliver that report to Congress by February 2006.

2.5 million veterans and their families. More than 176,000 women who received silicone breast implants filed suit against Dow Corning Company, which manufactured them. Some predict that asbestos litigation could eventually involve 1 to 3 million plaintiffs. The larger a mass-tort suit, the greater the chances that plaintiffs will have conflicting interests. That occurred in the asbestos litigation, where a relatively small number of plaintiffs who were already sick were put in the same class with a much larger group who had not yet developed symptoms. The Supreme Court twice rejected proposed settlements on the grounds that the lower courts should not have treated the asbestos plaintiffs as a single class.

> • **Do you favor a special court for malpractice cases? Would such a court be fair to patients?**

## Plaintiffs' lawyers are too powerful.

Tort reformers complain that the legal system has created a class of trial lawyers who earn excessive fees for their work. In the litigation by state governments against the tobacco industry, the tobacco companies agreed to pay the states 250 billion dollars to cover smoking-related health-care costs. Stephen Moore, the president of the pro-reform Club for Growth, argued that the trial lawyers in that case received windfall profits: "In that deal, a small gang of several hundred trial lawyers walked off with settlement money of an estimated $10 to $15 billion. If you filled Madison Square Garden with people who made $1 million, their total wealth would be slightly less than what the trial lawyers received in these settlements."[27] Critics also accuse trial lawyers of having become a powerful special interest bent on enriching itself. Author Max Boot remarked:

> I've yet to meet anybody willing to defend the current civil
> justice system who doesn't benefit from it, either directly (as
> is the case with all practicing lawyers, even those who never

enter a courtroom) or indirectly (Naderites get donations to their nonprofit groups from trial lawyers; law professors receive fat consulting fees from litigants).[28]

Trial lawyers have contributed millions of dollars to political candidates who oppose tort reform. In the 2000 election cycle, the Association of Trial Lawyers of America (ATLA) contributed 2.6 million dollars, more than twice what auto companies gave candidates. In states where judges are elected, trial lawyers give generously to candidates; then, after the judges are elected, the lawyers practice in the judges' courts. Critics call that practice "legalized bribery."

———•———————•———————•———

## Summary

Changes to the law, intended to give victims a better chance to recover from wrongdoers, have triggered an explosion of lawsuits. Laws that expand the right to sue and the erosion of rules that forbid lawyers to market their services have encouraged Americans to sue. The growing number of suits has impeded economic growth and created a class of trial lawyers who have turned litigation against deep-pockets defendants into a lucrative business. Those lawyers have filed class-action and mass-tort cases that sometimes benefit themselves at the expense of their clients. They have also used their earnings to lobby lawmakers, influence elections, and finance suits against new defendants.

# Litigation Is Not a Serious Problem

**B**usinesses and insurance companies have spent hundreds of millions of dollars to persuade Americans that litigation is out of control. Their efforts have paid off. As journalist Stephanie Mencimer noted, "There's very little that journalists won't repeat and readers won't swallow about the evils of the civil liability system." [29] Mencimer and others accuse reformers of exaggerating the litigation problem in an effort to frighten lawmakers into passing unnecessary restrictions on lawsuits. Responding to a *Newsweek* story about "lawsuit hell," she observed:

> Every few months, one or another newspaper, magazine, or television show does a story just like it. They all hew to a standard line, starting with a juicy but misleading—or even fictitious— lawsuit horror story typically describing an irresponsible

plaintiff, followed by "studies" on the economic damage of the tort system published by corporate front groups, finally ending with calls for "reforms" to rein in mushy-headed juries and greedy trial lawyers.[30]

---

• **Do Americans regard suing as a last resort? Does our society provide adequate alternatives to litigation?**

---

## There is no "litigation explosion."

According to David Clark, a professor at Willamette University Law School, "American civil justice might have serious problems, but an explosion of cases is no longer one of them."[31] The NCSC recently reported that personal-injury and tort filings, when adjusted to reflect population growth, have fallen by 8 percent since 1975. The data also show that tort cases are not the reason for the alleged "litigation explosion." In the 17 states that were able to provide data on both tort and contract filings, tort cases fell by 5 percent but contract cases rose by 21 percent between 1993 and 2001. Experts believe that many of those contract cases were filed by corporations to collect debts from consumers.

Furthermore, stories about "junk" lawsuits are exaggerated. Much has been written about obese people who sued the fast-food industry for allegedly making them fat. Only a handful of such suits were filed, however, and none have gone to trial. Author and lawyer Steven Brill, who began writing about litigation myths in the 1980s, contends that many junk-lawsuit stories are "urban legends" repeated by reporters who fail to check their facts.

Studies contradict the claim that Americans are litigious. According to Thomas Burke, a professor of political science at Wellesley College, only 2 percent of Americans who are injured in accidents, one-eighth of those injured by medical malpractice, and 5 percent of those who experience discrimination at work actually file suit. People rarely sue "on principle," because the potential recovery must be large enough to make the effort worthwhile. Even when a plaintiff decides to sue, his or her case might result in a potential recovery so small that no lawyer will take it. In any event, filing a suit is no guarantee of winning. Bureau of Justice Statistics data show that, in 2001, juries found for the plaintiff 52 percent of the time in civil cases in general and only 27 percent of the time in malpractice cases.

## Substantial reform has already taken place.

Since the 1970s, state lawmakers have taken steps to reduce the cost of lawsuits. That is especially true of malpractice cases. One of the earliest reforms occurred in 1975: California's Medical Injury Compensation Reform Act (MICRA),[32] which imposed a $250,000 limit on noneconomic damages in malpractice cases. Since then, most states have adopted similar limits, although the cap is often higher than $250,000. Some states have passed more comprehensive tort-reform laws. In 1995, the Texas legislature passed a law that included a cap on punitive damage awards in all lawsuits and limits on joint and several liability, a rule that applies if there is more than one defendant. Each defendant is potentially liable for the entire award of damages, regardless of how much it was at fault.

At the federal level, the Supreme Court addressed the problem of "junk science" by deciding *Daubert* v. *Merrell Dow Pharmaceuticals, Inc.*, 509 U.S. 579 (1993). That decision instructed judges to act as "gatekeepers" and reject unreliable expert testimony. The *Daubert* standard has been incorporated into the Federal Rules of Evidence: Rule 702 requires that "(1) the [expert] testimony is based upon sufficient facts or data, (2) the testimony is the product of reliable principles and methods, and (3) the witness has applied the principles and methods reliably to the facts of the case."[33] It has also addressed punitive-damage awards, ruling in *State Farm Mutual Automobile Insurance Company* v. *Campbell*, 538 U.S. 408 (2003), that a punitive award more than four times compensatory damages would likely be found unconstitutional.

## The cost of litigation is under control.

Tort reformers often cite Tillinghast–Towers Perrin's conclusion
that tort litigation costs our economy 246 billion dollars per
year. The consumer group Americans for Insurance Reform
(AIR) contends, however, that the figure is exaggerated: "Had
Tillinghast honestly measured tort system costs, these costs
would have been lower, by at least 50 percent, because so much
of what the company measures is not even vaguely related to the
legal system."[34]

> • **Are insurance companies telling the truth about the cost
> of lawsuits?**

AIR points out that the Tillinghast data include payments to
policyholders involved in traffic crashes, which generally do not
result in lawsuits, as well as insurance companies' overhead.
Other studies also rebut claims that tort costs are out of control.
A 1999 survey by Ernst & Young and the Risk and Insurance
Management Society found that companies paid only $5.20 in
liability costs for every $1,000 in revenue, and those costs had
fallen 37 percent since 1992. In January 2004, the Congressional
Budget Office reported that malpractice-related costs accounted
for less than 2 percent of overall health-care spending.

Many Americans believe that huge verdicts are more
common than they really are. That is in part because of media
coverage of civil cases. An article in the *Los Angeles Times*
referred to what Mark Galanter, a professor at the University
of Wisconsin, called "media distortion." In other words, huge
verdicts make news, small verdicts do not:

> [Galanter] cites studies of newspapers and magazines during
> the 1990s to illustrate the point. A study over six years in the
> New York area found the median jury award to be $250,000.
> However, during the same period, the median of the jury
> awards in the New York Times and New York Newsday was
> $4.3 million.[35]

What the media seldom report is that judges often reduce jury awards after the trial. A study by the Rand Corporation's Institute for Civil Justice found that, on average, judges reduced jury awards to 71 percent of the original amount. That figure fell to 57 percent when the award was larger than 10 million dollars.

# FROM THE BENCH

## The Case of the Spilled Coffee:
### *Liebeck* v. *McDonald's Corporation*

*Liebeck* v. *McDonald's Corporation* is one of the most famous tort cases in American history. It quickly became part of our national folklore and, for many, the symbol of a civil justice system run amok. (There is even a Website that hands out "Stella Awards" to recognize the most year's most frivolous lawsuits.) Defenders of the legal system maintain that justice was done in this case.

In February 1992, Stella Liebeck, a 79-year-old grandmother from Albuquerque, bought a cup of coffee at a McDonald's drive-through window. Her grandson, who was driving, parked the car so she could add cream and sugar to her coffee. She placed the cup between her knees and, while trying to remove the lid, spilled the coffee on her lap. Liebeck was wearing sweatpants, which absorbed the coffee and held it against her skin. She suffered severe burns and spent eight days in the hospital; she also underwent skin grafts and had tissue surgically removed.

McDonald's took a hard line. Liebeck reportedly asked for $10,000, but the company offered her much less. She then filed suit in District Court in Albuquerque. Days before the trial, a mediator recommended that McDonald's settle the case for $225,000. The company decided to go to trial instead.

At the beginning of the trial, jury foreman Jerry Goens wondered why he had to decide a hot coffee–spill case. Goens changed his mind when he saw the evidence. Like many franchise companies, McDonald's maintains strict control over its stores. The company's training manual called for coffee to be brewed at 195 to 205 degrees—almost boiling—and held at 180 to 190 degrees for optimal taste. A law student who worked for Liebeck's lawyer took temperatures of the coffee at other local restaurants and found that McDonald's coffee was at least 20 degrees warmer than coffee elsewhere. Documents revealed that company officials knew the coffee was dangerously hot but refused to do anything about it.

• **Should judges, rather than juries, determine damages in civil cases?**

Studies show that punitive-damage awards are rare. According to the Bureau of Justice Statistics for 2001, juries awarded them to only 2.7 percent of winning plaintiffs; furthermore, they

Witnesses testified that McDonald's had received more than 700 reports of customers being burned by hot coffee, that some incidents involved third-degree burns, and that it had been sued before over coffee spills. A quality assurance manager testified that the company did not intend to reduce the temperature of its coffee because "there were more serious dangers in restaurants." In addition, an expert hired by the company testified that hot-coffee burns were "statistically insignificant." That remark offended jurors, one of whom said, "There was a person behind every number and I don't think the corporation was attaching enough importance to that."

The jury quickly agreed that McDonald's was liable. It awarded Liebeck $200,000 in compensatory damages but found her 20 percent at fault for spilling the coffee on herself, thus reducing her award to $160,000. It also found that McDonald's had engaged in "willful, reckless, malicious or wanton" conduct, justifying an award of punitive damages. Following her lawyer's suggestion, it awarded Liebeck 2.7 million dollars, the equivalent of two days' worth of chainwide coffee sales by McDonald's.

After the trial, the judge reduced the punitive-damages portion of the award to $480,000, or three times Liebeck's compensatory damages, for a revised total of $640,000. Rather than risk an appeal, the two sides decided to settle. Because the settlement was secret, only the parties and their lawyers know for certain how much McDonald's ultimately paid. Observers agree that she received far less than what the jury awarded her.

Sources: American Trial Lawyers Association document, "McDonald's Scalding Coffee Case," available at *http://www.atlanet.org/ConsumerMediaResources/Tier3/press_room/ FACTS/frivolous/McdonaldsCoffeecase.aspx*; Andrea Garlin, "How Hot Do You Like It?," *Wall Street Journal*, September 1, 1994.

Stella Liebeck, a 79-year-old grandmother, became famous when she was awarded 2.7 million dollars after she accidentally spilled McDonald's coffee on her lap and suffered severe burns. Here, Liebeck looks on during a 1995 news conference to urge Congress to oppose the Common Sense Product Liability Legal Reform Act. President Clinton vetoed the bill in 1996.

awarded them more often in suits that alleged libel, slander, and intentional torts than in product-liability or malpractice cases. Large punitive awards were rarer still: During 2001, juries in the nation's 75 largest jurisdictions awarded more than one million dollars in only 23 cases out of the nearly 8,000 that went to trial. As in the case of compensatory damages, jury awards of punitive awards were often reduced later. In fact, Neal Vidmar, a professor at New York University, found that the larger the award, the steeper the discount. "Large malpractice verdicts in New York were typically reduced to between 5% and 10% of the original verdict amount. One case with a total award of $90.3 million was settled for $7 million. Another award, for $65.1 million, was reduced to $3.2 million." [36]

Finally, there is evidence that class-action litigation is not out of control. A study by law professors Theodore Eisenberg of Cornell and Geoffrey Miller of New York University found that both the average price of settling class-action suits and the average fee paid to class-action lawyers have held steady for ten years. The professors observed, "Contrary to popular belief, we find no robust evidence that either recoveries for plaintiffs or fees for their attorneys as a percentage of the class recovery increased" and that "neither the mean nor the median level of fee awards has increased over time." [37]

> • **Do you favor a uniform federal products liability law? A uniform federal law governing malpractice suits?**

## Tort law has adapted to a changing society.

Critics of tort reform argue that the justice system is functioning as intended—namely, by adapting long-standing legal principles to an age of mass-produced and mass-marketed products. Investigative reporter Dan Zegart argued:

> For now, the sheer scale of the harm done to an entire society by a defective mass-marketed product makes the

availability of the tort action essential, even while under-
lining its inadequacies: 11 million workers exposed to
asbestos, 10,000 children born with defects due to thalidomide,
1.5 million Pintos recalled, more than 6 million dieters who
used Phen Fen, which damaged the heart muscle. These are
truly modern plagues.[38]

# FROM THE BENCH

## Keeping "Junk Science" out of the Courtroom: *Daubert* v. *Merrell Dow Pharmaceuticals*

Legal experts believe that *Daubert* v. *Merrell Dow Pharmaceuticals*, 509 U.S. 579 (1993), has helped keep "junk science" out of the courtroom. That case began when the parents of Jason Daubert and Eric Schuller, who were born with serious birth defects, sued Merrell Dow Pharmaceuticals, Inc. Their lawsuit alleged that Merrell Dow's prescription anti-nausea drug, Benedictin, caused their children's birth defects.

The District Court concluded that Benedictin did not cause birth defects in humans and entered summary judgment for Merrell Dow. Its conclusion was based on an affidavit by Merrell Dow's expert, who had reviewed the published studies on Benedictin and concluded that none linked the drug to birth defects. The court rejected the Benedictin studies offered by the plaintiffs' experts. It did so because they had not been published or subjected to peer review—scrutiny by others in the same field—and therefore did not satisfy the standard laid down in *Frye* v. *United States*, 293 F. 1013 (D.C. Cir. 1923). *Frye* held that expert testimony based on a scientific technique could not be admitted unless it was "generally accepted" as reliable in the scientific community.

At the time, the federal appeals courts were divided as to whether *Frye* still applied. The 9th Circuit, which followed *Frye*, affirmed the District Court's judgment. The Daubert and Schuller families appealed to the Supreme Court, which unanimously ruled that the Federal Rules of Evidence, adopted in 1975, overrode the *Frye* standard. Justice Harry Blackmun wrote the majority opinion.

Justice Blackmun found that Rule 702, which governed expert testimony, replaced the rigid *Frye* standard with a more flexible one. That rule authorized a judge to admit expert testimony if the expert's scientific, technical, or other specialized knowledge would "assist the trier of fact to understand the evidence

Author and lawyer Jay Feinman offered an example. For decades, doctors prescribed the drug diethylstilbestrol (DES) to pregnant women to prevent miscarriage. Tests linked DES to bladder cancer in the daughters of women who used it, and drug companies allegedly kept marketing it although they should have known about the risk of cancer. Had the courts

or to determine a fact in issue" and if, "by knowledge, skill, experience, training, or education," he or she qualified as an expert.

Although Rule 702 did not impose a rigid "generally accepted" test, Justice Blackmun concluded that it still required the trial judge to act as a "gatekeeper." Before admitting scientific evidence, the judge had to make a preliminary determination that it was relevant (intended to resolve the issues in the case), reliable (capable of producing consistent results), and based on scientific reasoning. Blackmun identified several factors that the judge should consider, including whether others could test the expert's methods, whether the expert's findings had been published and subject to peer review, how prone to errors the expert's methods were, and whether the expert's findings had been accepted by the scientific community—still an important consideration. Justice Blackmun also noted that "there are important differences between the quest for truth in the courtroom and the quest for truth in the laboratory"; therefore, conjecture that was probably wrong had little value as evidence.

Justice Blackmun added that there were other safeguards against the admission of unreliable scientific evidence. Rule 706 authorized the judge to find an expert of his own choosing, and Rule 403 barred the admission of evidence whose relevance was outweighed by the danger of prejudice or confusion. He added that "vigorous cross-examination, presentation of contrary evidence, and careful instruction on the burden of proof are the traditional and appropriate means of attacking shaky but admissible evidence."

Although Rule 702 applies only to trials in federal courts, most state courts have adopted some version of the *Daubert* standard.

followed traditional rules of causation and damages, it might have been impossible for the "DES daughters" to recover. The courts altered the proof requirements in two ways: First, they allowed the DES daughters to offer statistical evidence that tended to show that DES, as opposed to some other factor, caused their cancer. Second, because of the difficulty of proving who made the drug the mothers took, they allowed the DES daughters to recover on the basis of "market share liability": Drug companies' liability was based on their share of the DES market at the time the drug was taken. Critics called this approach "judicial legislation," but Feinman called it "debatable" but "traditionally judicial": The courts balanced the competing policies of tort law and arrived at what they considered just compensation.[39]

It has also been argued that lawsuits are a consequence of living in a modern, complex society. Authors Quentin Johnston and Dan Hopson offered several reasons why Americans resort to the courts: Our nation's wealth, its greater social disorganization, a tradition of insisting that government and corporations act fairly, and a belief that bureaucracies are incompetent or corrupt and thus courts should act as a check on them.[40] Some argue that certain litigation is a welcome by-product of society's commitment to justice. Jon Robins, a contributor to the British magazine *The Lawyer*, observed, "Indeed, the 'onslaught of litigation' over the past 30 years decried in *Newsweek* is a relative term. In 1962, for instance, only about 300 civil rights lawsuits were filed in federal courts. In 2000 there were more than 40,000—an onslaught, to be sure, but that's because prior to 1964 racial discrimination was legal."[41]

## Summary

Defenders of the civil justice system accuse tort reformers of creating the false impression that lawsuits are out of control.

They claim that reformers use misleading data about clogged court dockets and exaggerated stories about "junk" lawsuits. Defenders cite studies that show that there has been no "litigation explosion," that the biggest increase in filings has been by corporations, and that "jackpot" judgments are less common than people think. They also point out that, over the past 30 years, courts and lawmakers have taken steps to rein in excessive verdicts and to keep "junk science" out of the courtroom.

# Lawsuits Are Unfair to Both Businesses and Consumers

**W**alter Olson summarized tort reformers' complaints about the courts' pro-plaintiff drift in the late twentieth century:

> Liberalization of pretrial discovery in the 1970s made it easier for lawyers to go on so-called fishing expeditions, hoping that the contents of their opponents' filing cabinets would contain something, anything, justifying their suit. "Long-arm" jurisdiction made it easier for litigants to shop around for a court and juries convenient to them or hostile to their opponent. And, symbolically, old ideas of legal ethics were fast being overturned.[42]

The result, according to Olson and other reformers, is a civil justice system in which corporate defendants, especially those with deep pockets, can no longer expect to receive a fair trial.

## Lawsuits diminish the quality of life.

Litigation was a major factor in the removal of intrauterine devices (IUDs) and Norplant rods, two forms of birth control, from the American market. The Manhattan Institute observed that "only three new contraceptive products have come to market in the U.S. in the last decade, all of them variations on existing technology; not surprisingly, American companies today spend 20 times more on developing new cosmetics than on research into contraceptives."[43] The problem is not limited to the health-care industry: Products ranging from sporting equipment to small planes to automobiles have either been driven off the market or not introduced because of fear of liability.

When courts and lawmakers expanded the right to sue, they had good intentions—namely, to give Americans more protection against arbitrary treatment. Unfortunately, the "due process revolution" has had the unintended consequence of creating what lawyer and tort-reform activist Philip Howard has called a "climate of fear":

> The fear of litigation began to hang over ordinary daily choices. Every school, hospital, church, and sporting league knew of lawsuits for what were once ordinary accidents and disputes. It did not matter who won or lost, or even if the likelihood of being sued were small. The fact that any self-interested person could unilaterally sue for almost every injury or gripe meant that people no longer felt free to do what they believed was right.[44]

Howard added, "Our society has been changed in a subtler, sadder way. We have been hardened and made more fearful. Friends and neighbors are more wary now. Almost anyone has to ask: if I say or do something that might be taken wrong, will I wind up in court?"[45]

In fact, reformers contend that tort liability has expanded to the point that many individuals find themselves facing a legal catch-22:

An employer now faces a lawsuit from victims if it lets a suspected-but-not-proven drug abuser stay in a safety-related position, and a lawsuit from the worker if it does not. A clinic counselor fears an invasion-of-privacy lawsuit if he warns a client's wife that her husband is infected with the AIDS virus, and a failure-to-warn lawsuit if he does not. Athletic doctors have been sued alike for ordering

## Proposed Common Sense Product Liability Act of 1996

Before medical malpractice and asbestos cases took center stage, product liability was a top priority of tort reformers. Congress responded to calls for reform by passing H.R. 956, 104th Congress, the Common Sense Product Liability Legal Reform Act of 1996, which would have imposed uniform national standards in product liability cases. President Clinton vetoed the bill.

Major provisions of the act included these:

- Section 103(a). Bars lawsuits against the innocent seller of a defective product.

- Section 103(c). Bars suits against the lessor of a product, such as a car, where the only basis for the suit is the fact that the lessor owned the product.

- Section 104. Disqualifies a plaintiff from recovering if he or she was injured while under the influence of alcohol or drugs, and if his or her intoxication was more than 50 percent responsible for the injuries.

- Section 105. Reduces a plaintiff's recovery by the extent to which he or she contributed to his or her injuries by misusing the product, or by the extent to which the injuries were caused by a risk he or she knew or should have known about.

- Section 106(a). Requires a plaintiff to file suit no later than two years after he or she either discovered his or her injuries or should have discovered them.

their patients not to take part in big games . . . and for letting them play in cases where they then collapse on the playing field.[46]

> • **Should nonprofit organizations such as the Boy Scouts be immune from lawsuits?**

- Section 106(b). Establishes a "statute of repose" under which a plaintiff may not sue later than 15 years after the product was first delivered to the original buyer or lessee. States may establish a period shorter than 15 years. The statute of repose does not apply to mass-transit vehicles such as buses or trains, or to products covered by an express warranty for a longer period.

- Section 107. Entitles a defendant, within 60 days after being sued, to offer to send the case to alternative dispute resolution.

- Section 108(a). Allows punitive damages only in cases where the plaintiff proves, by clear and convincing evidence, that his or her injuries resulted from the defendant's "conscious, flagrant indifference to the rights or safety of others."

- Section 108(b). Limits punitive damages to twice the plaintiff's compensatory damages or $250,000, whichever amount is greater. A judge may award a larger amount if he or she concludes it is necessary to punish the defendant for "egregious conduct." If the defendant's net worth is less than $500,000 or if it has fewer than 25 full-time employees, punitive damages are limited to twice the plaintiff's compensatory damages or $250,000, whichever amount is less.

- Section 110. Limits a defendant's liability for non-economic damages to the percentage to which he or she was found at fault. In allocating fault, the court must consider everyone whose actions contributed to the plaintiff's injuries, whether they are defendants or not.

## Courts make arbitrary and illogical decisions.

Tort reformers argue that courts have abandoned traditional standards that require a plaintiff to prove that the defendant caused injuries and the amount of the damages. They add that liberal rules of pleading make it too difficult for judges to dispose of weak cases.

Reformers also criticize noneconomic damages, in part because the standards that govern them are so vague that the results are arbitrary: "Unlike economic damages . . . the amount of pain and suffering damages awarded depends only on the jury's subjective judgment. As a result, sympathetic plaintiffs represented by skillful lawyers are often awarded higher levels of compensation than other victims with similar injuries."[47]

Punitive damages are considered even more objectionable because there are fewer restraints. Juries often work without clear guidelines, awards are larger than most criminal fines, and a defendant is subject to multiple awards that result from the same conduct. Because juries can consider the defendant's wealth, the largest damage awards are directed at unlucky deep-pockets defendants, not the worst wrongdoers. Some reformers, like Philip Howard, question whether punitive damages even deter wrongdoing. He observed, "Trial lawyers claim that punitive damages are a disincentive to bad conduct. But since they're unpredictable and arbitrary, they are more of a disincentive to do anything but settle a case."[48]

Because tort law varies across states, plaintiffs' lawyers look for the friendliest place in which to file suit. This "forum shopping" is possible because many states have broad standards of jurisdiction. At one time, a defendant could be sued only in his home state. In later years, however, the Supreme Court has allowed state courts to exercise jurisdiction over out-of-state defendants. Some states have gone farther and allowed out-of-state plaintiffs to file suit in their courts.

> • **Is it fair that trial lawyers can choose where to file suit? Should the law be more uniform across states?**

Today, there are a handful of jurisdictions whose courts unfairly favor plaintiffs. They have liberal rules of procedure and judges who allow dubious legal theories, discovery abuse, and junk science. The American Tort Reform Association (ATRA) calls them "judicial hellholes." In 2003 and 2004, Madison County, Illinois, was named the nation's worst hellhole. One reason is the willingness of its judges to certify cases as class actions—a decision that all but guarantees a settlement, however weak the plaintiff's case might be. Between 1998 and 2003, the number of class-action suits filed there increased by 5,000 percent, and many plaintiffs in those suits had no connection with the county. One suit, which accused Philip Morris USA of fraudulently claiming that its "light" cigarettes were "safer," resulted in a 10.1-billion-dollar judgment. Trial lawyer Dickie Scruggs once said of jurisdictions like Madison County, "It's almost impossible to get a fair trial if you're a defendant in some of these places. The plaintiff lawyer walks in there and writes the number on the blackboard, and the first juror meets the last one coming out the door with that amount of money."[49]

## Tort law leads to bad public policy.

Reformers contend that tort law has been stretched beyond its original intent to compensate those injured by wrongdoers. They accuse trial lawyers of using the law as a means of expressing public outrage or, even worse, as an "end run" around the political process. Some are especially critical of litigation against the makers of federally approved products such as prescription drugs; they contend that it "directly undermines the FDA's congressional mandate to approve which drugs are safe and effective enough to be sold."[50] Trial lawyers have also been accused of using the legal process to impose regulations on legal products such as tobacco, guns, and fast food, even though lawmakers have already created mechanisms for regulating these. Federal appeals judge Paul Niemeyer observed, "We have never been able to regulate tobacco in Congress, yet it has been regulated in the courts. Class actions can accomplish a lot, but the question is why is the class action accomplishing it as opposed to Congress or the state legislatures."[51]

> • **Will lawsuits against legal products, such as fast food and guns, result in their being taken off the market? Should Congress ban those suits?**

Finally, some litigation allegedly makes the public less safe and thus does more harm than good. Health-care professionals argue that malpractice suits create a "culture of blame" that hinders efforts to improve the quality of care:

> Far from encouraging transparency in health care, our adversarial legal system has normalized hiding information about risk. Victim's rights advocates continue to express intolerance for error that is totally inconsistent with a scientific understanding of human and complex system performance yet are much too lenient in accepting the sealing of court records when cases are settled.[52]

## The civil justice system is inefficient.

Reformers argue that the civil justice system is plagued by high "transaction costs," meaning that it is both expensive and time consuming to use the courts to resolve disputes. The Tillinghast consulting firm found that "the U.S. tort system is highly inefficient, returning less than 50 cents on the dollar to the people it is designed to help and returning only 22 cents to compensate for actual economic loss."[53] One reason

Doctors and other supporters gathered at a rally to support tort reform at the Capitol in Jackson, Mississippi, on April 28, 2004. Professionals in the health care industry argue that malpractice suits create a "culture of blame" that is an obstacle to efforts to improve health care.

transaction costs are so high is the excessive fees paid to lawyers, especially in class-action suits. A shareholders' suit against Cendant Corporation resulted in a multibillion-dollar settlement that included an award of 262 million dollars in

## Asbestos Litigation: Do Mass-Tort Cases Belong in the Courts?

A controversial area of tort law is mass-tort litigation, in which thousands, even millions, of plaintiffs claim that they were injured by the same product or action. One of the longest and most complex mass-tort cases of all time involves asbestos, a substance used to make products stronger and more heat-resistant. It was used in building materials and auto parts. Those who were exposed to it ran the risk of contracting asbestosis, a disease of the lungs that often proves fatal. Symptoms of the disease often do not appear until many years after the victim was exposed to it.

The first asbestos lawsuit was filed in 1966. That case was unsuccessful, but lawyers eventually began to win cases against the asbestos industry. The litigation gained momentum after plaintiffs' lawyers discovered documents that showed that, as early as the 1930s, asbestos manufacturers knew about the dangers of their product and allegedly conspired to keep that knowledge from the public. Evidence of a cover-up triggered lawsuits that alleged fraud, which led to awards of punitive damages.

Because asbestos was so widely used, millions of Americans were exposed to it, especially at work. The result was a flood of lawsuits, first by those who worked at asbestos plants; next by workers exposed in shipyards, refineries, and power plants; and then by construction workers who used products that contained asbestos.

The potential liability from lawsuits grew so large that, in the 1980s, asbestos makers began to file for bankruptcy. Plaintiffs' lawyers then pursued other companies, such as the owners of refineries and power plants and makers of products that contained asbestos. So far, more than 75 companies have gone bankrupt on account of asbestos liability. Many employees of those companies lost their jobs and pensions, and many shareholders suffered heavy losses.

About 850,000 asbestos-related lawsuits have been filed so far, including more than 100,000 in 2003 alone. All of these plaintiffs allege that they were exposed to fees, which came out to more than $10,000 an hour. What made the case unusual was not the size of the award—hourly fees have reportedly ranged as high as $25,000—but the fact that one of the plaintiffs' lawyers complained to the judge that

asbestos, but they fall into different classes: A small number who are seriously ill and a larger number who have not come down with a disease but who might in the future. These plaintiffs—and their lawyers—have conflicting interests. Some argue that claims by those who have not yet gotten sick clog the courts and divert money from those who are seriously ill.

The size of the asbestos litigation and the defendants' potential liability, which some estimate at 200 billion dollars or more, has created powerful pressure to settle. The rules of procedure that govern class-action suits prevented that from happening. In the early 1990s, all asbestos suits filed in federal court were sent to U.S. District Court in Philadelphia. Both sides attempted to settle the litigation, but the Supreme Court refused to accept the settlement. Although the Court applauded the efforts to settle, it rejected them because the class members lacked the commonality required by the rules. In *Amchem Products, Inc.* v. *Windsor,* 521 U.S. 591 (1997), Justice Stephen Breyer expressed his belief that there were better alternatives than class-action suits: "A nationwide administrative claims processing regime would provide the most secure, fair, and efficient means of compensating victims of asbestos exposure."[*] Later, in *Ortiz* v. *Fibreboard Corporation,* 527 U.S. 815 (1999), Chief Justice Rehnquist wrote that "the 'elephantine mass of asbestos cases'... cries out for a legislative solution."[**]

The Asbestos Alliance, an industry group, warns that unless Congress legislates a solution, more companies will go bankrupt and most of the money paid out by asbestos defendants could be paid to lawyers rather than to victims. Legislation that would have created a national trust fund, privately financed by asbestos companies and their insurers, died in the 108th Congress. The current Congress is considering a similar bill.

[*]   521 U.S. 591, 628-29 (1997) (Breyer, J., concurring in part).
[**]  527 U.S. 815, 865 (199) (Rehnquist, C.J., concurring).

the fees were too high. An appeals court pressured the lawyers to accept 55 million dollars. An editorial in the *Wall Street Journal* sharply criticized litigation such as the Cendant class action: "The companies involved pay a huge ransom to the trial bar, while shareholders watch the value of their holdings plummet, employees lose their jobs, or consumers pay more for goods and services once companies are forced to pay billions of dollars in settlements." [54]

> • **Should lawyer's fees be limited to, say, $250 an hour, regardless of the size of the award?**

At the same time that lawyers collect large fees, the class members themselves often wind up with little or nothing. In a suit against Blockbuster Entertainment Corporation that involved allegations of overcharges for late video returns, Blockbuster agreed to distribute 500 million dollars worth of coupons, each good for one dollar off a future rental. Most of the coupons were never redeemed, and Blockbuster kept the value of the unredeemed coupons. Nevertheless, the plaintiffs' lawyers received 9.25 million dollars in fees. The prospect of generous fees has encouraged trial lawyers to file even more class-action suits. Between 1997 and 2000, American corporations reported that federal class actions against them tripled and state class actions filed increased tenfold.

## Summary

Well-intentioned efforts to make the civil justice system fairer have triggered litigation that enriches trial lawyers but diminishes the quality of other Americans' lives. Lawsuits have driven legal and worthwhile products from the market and have made other products and services more expensive. The fear of lawsuits has even disrupted social relations. Today, judges and juries hand down arbitrary decisions, especially against corporations, which are often forced to pay judgments out of proportion to their wrongdoing. Some trial lawyers also use litigation to bring about social change without having to go through the political process.

# On Balance, Lawsuits Benefit Society

I n a case that involved the discipline of a lawyer, the Supreme Court commented on the importance of having one's "day in court":

> There is no cause for consternation when a person who believes in good faith and on the basis of accurate information regarding his legal rights that he has suffered a legally cognizable injury turns to the courts for a remedy: we cannot accept the notion that it is always better for a person to suffer a wrong silently than to redress it by legal action. That our citizens have access to their civil courts is not an evil to be regretted; rather, it is an attribute of our system of justice in which we ought to take pride.[55]

Defenders of the civil justice system accuse reformers of tampering with Anglo-American rights that date back to the Magna Carta, signed nearly 800 years ago.

- **Are lawsuits a sign of a healthy society or one that is in decline?**

## Lawsuits discourage corporate wrongdoing.

What would happen if there were no tort liability? Jay Feinman speculated, "People would have less incentive to avoid injuring other people. . . . An auto manufacturer would have an incentive to cut back on safety measures if it knew it would not be liable for injuries that were caused by defective cars. Drivers might be less careful, and property owners might be less inclined to repair their sidewalks."[56]

Furthermore, many believe that compensatory damages alone do not give corporations enough incentive to act in the public's best interest. They warn that, without stronger measures, executives might engage in "Pinto math." That term refers to Ford Motor Company's alleged decision to market the Pinto automobile, despite the danger that occupants would be killed or injured in postcrash fires, because it would be cheaper to pay damage awards than to make the needed design changes. A California appeals court, which upheld a 3.5-million-dollar punitive-damage award against Ford in a lawsuit brought by a Pinto fire victim, explained why such an award was appropriate:

> In the traditional noncommercial intentional tort, compensatory damages alone may serve as an effective deterrent against future wrongful conduct but in commerce-related torts, the manufacturer may find it more profitable to treat compensatory damages as a part of the cost of doing business rather than to remedy the defect. . . . Governmental safety standards and the criminal law have

failed to provide adequate consumer protection against the manufacture and distribution of defective products. . . . Punitive damages thus remain as the most effective remedy for consumer protection against defectively designed mass produced articles.[57]

Some believe that the publicity that results from a damage award is an additional deterrent to wrongdoing and warn that tort reform would eliminate that "shame factor." Stephanie Mencimer pointed out that, although tort suits fell by 40 percent after the Texas legislature passed its 1995 tort-reform law, corporate wrongdoing did not fall by a corresponding amount—it simply received less publicity.

# THE LETTER OF THE LAW

## When Are Punitive-Damage Awards Proper?

Section 908 of the *Restatement (Second) of Torts* provides:

(1) "Punitive damages" are damages, other than compensatory or nominal damages, awarded against a person to punish him for his outrageous conduct.

(2) Punitive damages may be awarded for conduct that is outrageous, because of the defendant's evil motive or his reckless indifference to the rights of others. In assessing punitive damages, the trier of fact can properly consider the character of the defendant's act, the nature and extent of the harm to the plaintiff that the defendant caused or intended to cause and the wealth of the defendant.

Comment (b) accompanying this section indicates that punitive damages are awarded only for outrageous conduct, that is, acts committed with a bad motive or with reckless indifference to others' interests. Comment (c) notes that, in many cases, where a plaintiff is awarded compensatory damages for emotional distress, there is no clear line that separates punishment and compensation and that a verdict for a specified amount frequently includes elements of both.

• Do corporations treat damage awards as "just another cost of doing business"?

## Lawsuits have made products safer.

The rate of accidental death in the United States fell by more than 20 percent between 1975 and 2000, and many believe that lawsuits were a factor. A 1987 study of corporate risk managers conducted by the Conference Board, an organization of business executives, confirmed that belief: "Where product liability has had a notable impact—where it has most significantly affected management decision making—has been in the quality of the products themselves. Managers say products have been safer, manufacturing procedures have been improved, and labels and use instructions have become more explicit."[58] According to an ATLA report, nearly 80 percent of punitive-damages awards against manufacturers resulted in the defendant making a safety change to the product involved. Because of lawsuits, asbestos was taken off the market, football helmets were made safer, manufacturers recalled superabsorbent tampons linked to toxic shock syndrome, and Domino's Pizza dropped its "30 minutes or free" guarantee, which encouraged unsafe driving.

Trial lawyers also maintain that malpractice suits are needed to make our health-care system safer. A 1999 study by the federal government's Institute of Medicine found that medical errors kill as many as 98,000 Americans per year, more than twice as many as die in vehicle crashes. Many of those deaths were preventable. According to Dr. Sidney Wolfe, the director of Public Citizen's Health Research Group, 5 percent of the nation's doctors are responsible for more than half of all malpractice claims, and many are repeat offenders who are not adequately disciplined by the medical profession. Trial lawyers argue that, because the medical profession has not done enough to police itself, it is necessary for the courts to step in and impose standards that protect patients from incompetent doctors.

At a time when lawmakers are rolling back regulations and cutting agency budgets, some argue that the tort system is an essential "last line of defense" to protect the public. Consider the example of Vioxx, an antiarthritis drug approved by the FDA. In late 2004, it was reported that Merck and Company continued to market the drug even though studies showed that it increased the risk of heart attacks and strokes and that the FDA was reluctant to take Vioxx off the market because it was a "high-profile" medication. An editorial in the *St. Petersburg Times* stated, "With $2.5 billion in Vioxx sales last year, Merck could emerge as Exhibit A for those who argue sizable damage awards are needed to curb gigantic corporations seeking profit while concealing risks to customers." [59]

> • Is the health care system doing enough to police itself?
>   What can be done to make it safer?

## Tort reform is unfair to deserving victims.

Trial lawyers remind us that all Americans are equal under the law and that the courtroom is a forum where the average person can fight a multinational corporation on even terms. Todd Smith, the president of ATLA, explained, "The real genius of our system is that you don't have to have political power . . . to have your claim adjudicated in a fair system. . . . That is what makes our civil system, in my opinion, the envy of the world." [60]

Smith and others accuse tort reformers of trying to close the courts to ordinary Americans by limiting damage awards and lawyers' fees and by reimposing strict rules of procedure. They are especially critical of limits on trial by jury. In their view, damage caps interfere with a centuries-old function of the jury—namely, determining the amount of the plaintiff's injuries. In some states, appeals courts have agreed with them and found caps unconstitutional. Trial lawyers also accuse reformers of portraying jurors as unfair and uninformed. One of them, Jeffrey White, responded, "Juries follow the court's instructions conscientiously and base their decisions on evidence rather than emotion. Their decisions are generally in line with what judges or professional arbitrators would have decided, demonstrating that juries are capable of doing justice in even complex cases."[61] Some lawyers charge reformers with appealing to bigotry by using terms such as "hellhole" to describe jurisdictions with large minority populations.

Trial lawyers warn that tort-reform measures will deprive deserving victims of their day in court. They contend that rules aimed at curbing "junk science" require them to spend $100,000 or more to win a personal-injury case, especially one that involves malpractice. The cost of proving liability forces them to turn down clients whose case is worth less than a million dollars; as a result, plaintiffs with small and medium-sized claims are shut out of court. Caps on noneconomic damages—in particular, pain and suffering—compound the problem, especially when the victim is a child, a retiree, or a stay-at-home parent. In California, which has had a $250,000 cap on noneconomic damages in malpractice cases since 1975, trial lawyer Donald Costello told the *Wall Street Journal* about two of his clients' cases, both of which involved mothers in their 40s who died of breast cancer. The family of one, a Silicon Valley executive, recovered 3 million dollars; the other family received only $300,000 because the woman did not work outside the home. The case involving the executive resulted in a substantially larger award because it included her economic damages, which were not capped. Her economic damages were based on how much she would have earned at work had she not died.

Finally, trial lawyers accuse tort reformers of being callous about pain and suffering. As Todd Smith argued, "Noneconomic damages are the only compensation a jury may provide for actual life-altering injuries like blindness, paraplegia, loss of limbs, loss of fertility, gross disfigurement, the death of a child or the abuse of a parent in a nursing home. These are anything but trivial or frivolous injuries."[62]

## FROM THE BENCH

### The Pinto Case: *Grimshaw v. Ford Motor Company*

In 1968, Ford Motor Company began to design a new subcompact car called the Pinto. Its top management was determined to build a car that weighed no more than 2,000 pounds and to do it cheaply enough that it could be sold for $2,000 or less. Working under budget and time constraints, company engineers designed a car that was prone to leak fuel and catch fire after a rear-end collision. According to internal documents, design changes that cost four to eight dollars would have made the car safer. Top management postponed making those changes, allegedly because it would be cheaper to pay damages to crash victims than to make the car safer.

One victim was Lilly Gray, whose Pinto was rear-ended on a California freeway after it unexpectedly stalled. The resulting fire caused Gray's death; her 13-year-old passenger, Richard Grimshaw, was disfigured by the flames and required years of reconstructive surgery. His family sued Ford. A Superior Court jury awarded the Grimshaws 2,516,000 dollars in compensatory damages and 125 million dollars in punitive damages. The judge reduced the punitive-damage award to 3.5 million dollars. Both sides appealed.

In *Grimshaw v. Ford Motor Company*, 119 Cal. App. 3d 757, 174 Cal. Rptr. 348 (Cal. Ct. App. 1981), the District Court of Appeal affirmed the 3.5-million-dollar award. Justice Stephen Tamura wrote the court's opinion. He concluded that an award of punitive damages was appropriate in light of Ford executives'"callous and conscious disregard of public safety." Compensatory damages were enough to deter wrongdoing by average citizens, but he found that punitive damages were needed to deter large corporations from mass-marketing dangerous products.

Justice Tamura next concluded that the 3.5-million-dollar punitive-damage award was not excessive. Under California law, the factors to be weighed in deciding the reasonableness of an award included the defendant's wealth, the amount of compensatory damages, and whether the award would deter future wrongdoing. In this case, the punitive-damage award amounted to only 0.005 percent of Ford's

## The alternatives to tort law are worse.

Opponents of tort reform warn that some measures can produce consequences worse than the litigation itself. One example is a 1995 federal law that restricts shareholders' suits against

net worth and 0.03 percent of its 1976 net income and was only about 1.4 times the compensatory-damage award. Furthermore, an award "so small that it can be simply written off as a part of the cost of doing business" would have no deterrent effect. He responded to Ford's argument that the punitive-damage award was excessive because it was much larger than the maximum allowable fine for selling unsafe cars: "It is precisely because monetary penalties under government regulations prescribing business standards or the criminal law are so inadequate and ineffective as deterrents against a manufacturer and distributor of mass produced defective products that punitive damages must be of sufficient amount to discourage such practices."

Justice Tamura, however, rejected the Grimshaws' argument that the jury's original award of 125 million dollars should have allowed to stand. He pointed out such an award would have been 44 times compensatory damages and suggested that the trial judge had reduced the award because Ford might face punitive-damage awards in future Pinto cases.

A postscript: The verdict in *Grimshaw*, which was handed down shortly after a critical article appeared in *Mother Jones* magazine, led the federal government to resume its investigation of the car. In June 1978, Ford agreed to pay the cost of repairing 1.5 million Pintos. Before the necessary parts arrived at dealerships, six more people died in Pinto fires. Three were killed in an Indiana crash, which led to reckless homicide charges against Ford. Although the jury found the company not guilty of the criminal charges, it suffered additional bad publicity.

Trial lawyers cite the Pinto litigation as an example of how lawsuits forced manufacturers to make safer products. Some experts, however, believe that the legal system unfairly singled out the Pinto. Gary Schwartz, a law professor at UCLA, has argued that crash data showed the Pinto to be no more prone to fire than other cars of the time. He has also argued that the "smoking-gun" memo at the heart of the *Grimshaw* case pertained to cars in general, not specifically to the Pinto, and that Ford's analysis was similar to that used by federal safety regulators.

corporations. Some argue that the law took away the incentive for executives to follow proper accounting standards. As a result, Enron, WorldCom, and other companies engaged in unscrupulous accounting practices that cost their shareholders and employees billions of dollars and shook public confidence in corporate management.

It has also been argued that restricting lawsuits will not eliminate the costs associated with personal injuries. Billions of dollars will be needed to care for victims and replace their lost income, and those funds will have to come from somewhere— in many cases, the taxpayers. Furthermore, limits on lawsuits could cost society billions of dollars in added health-care costs and benefits for disabled victims if dangerous products return to the market and the quality of medical care deteriorates. Much of that burden will fall on innocent victims. It was for that reason that courts extended strict-tort liability to product-liability cases. As the *Greenman* court explained, it adopted strict liability "to insure that the costs of injuries resulting from defective products are borne by the manufacturers that put such products on the market rather than by the injured persons who are powerless to protect themselves."[63]

Finally, defenders of the civil justice system argue that, imperfect as it is, it is still better than the alternatives. Jay Feinman observed, "Consider what happens in subcultures in which litigation is unavailable. Among drug dealers, for example, disputes and claims of right are likely to be settled with drive-by shootings. But even aside from the threat of violence, the presence of unresolved grievances corrodes the public's sense of social order and well-being."[64] They point out that even the Tillinghast study concedes that lawsuits benefit the public by providing a means of resolving disputes and thus resolving larger conflicts.

- **Do you think our legal system is fairer than those of other countries?**

## Summary

Tort reformers unfairly downplay the benefits of the civil justice system. Lawsuits, the bad publicity that accompanies them, and the deterrent potential of punitive damages benefit society in the form of safer products and better corporate behavior. In an era of deregulation, the courts are the last line in defense that protects the public from harm. Tort law also shifts the burden of compensating the injured from the victims themselves to those who caused their injuries. Damage caps and other reform measures threaten long-standing American principles of equal justice under the law, trial by jury, and an independent judiciary.

# It Is Too Easy to Abuse the Legal System

Tort reformers contend that the intention of the civil justice system—to compensate victims—has been turned on its head. Today, innocent defendants are victims of abusive litigation: Wealthy corporations pay huge damage awards, and individual defendants, especially professionals such as doctors, find their reputations damaged. Philip Howard told a congressional committee, "A lawsuit is just like indicting someone, except that the penalty is money. The mere possibility of a lawsuit changes people's behavior."[65] Trial lawyers, however, are not ultimately accountable to voters, as prosecutors are, and civil defendants enjoy a lesser degree of constitutional protection than a person charged with a crime does.

> • Is it too easy to charge someone with a crime? Are there too many criminal laws on the books?

## There are too few checks on trial lawyers.

Unlike most other professionals, trial lawyers can use the coercive power of government to disrupt other people's lives. According to Walter Olson:

> They can charge opponents with shocking-sounding wrong-doing. . . . They can compel defendants to testify against themselves and pull new charges out of a hat at the last minute. They can bring a long line of plaintiffs to court to challenge the same underlying acts of a defendant, and if 10 juries find no guilt they can call on an 11th. At the end of it they can pocket for themselves and their clients fines of a magnitude with not much limit outside the indignant imagination.[66]

Despite their sweeping powers, there are few checks on them. Today's rules of civil procedure do little to restrain litigation. A century ago, the rules were so strict that judges could—and did—dismiss suits on a variety of grounds, even trivial mistakes in the pleadings. Some reformers argue that, although the old rules were harsh, they benefited the public by forcing lawyers to think twice before suing. Today, reformers maintain, the rules have gone too far in the direction of encouraging litigation. As Olson observed, "Fearful of being accused of pettifogging [nitpicking] specificity, the American courts instead made themselves into a place where nothing was secure and anything could happen. What began as a page out of Dickens ended as a page out of Kafka."[67]

Reformers point to other aspects of the legal system that invite abuse. They claim that contingent fees encourage unjust litigation in much the same way that ticket quotas for police officers invite unjust arrests. As the AMA pointed out, "Trial lawyers that link their payment to awards have an inherent incentive to generate as much litigation as possible and drag out proceedings as long as possible."[68] Reformers also blame the "American rule," which generally provides that the losing party does not have to pay the winner's legal fees, for encouraging lawsuits. For most plaintiffs, the worst possible outcome of a baseless lawsuit is that it will be dismissed; thus there is little downside to filing it. Because a defendant cannot recoup legal fees, however, he or she will be financially worse off than if he or she had not been sued in the first place.

## Mississippi Tackles Tort Reform

A few years ago, the United States Chamber of Commerce accused Mississippi of having the nation's "worst litigation environment," *Newsweek* described Holmes and Jefferson counties as the nation's worst venues for corporate defendants.

Tort reformers were especially critical of the state's liberal rules governing where a suit could be filed and who could be added to it. The rules allowed a trial lawyer to recruit a local plaintiff to file suit and then encourage out-of-state plaintiffs to join the case. A single lawsuit could attract hundreds, even thousands, of plaintiffs, many of whom had never set foot in Mississippi and whose individual claims were often quite different from one another's.

Reformers also criticized the state's generous rules governing damages. Because there were no limits on punitive or noneconomic damages, some cases generated huge, highly-publicized verdicts that gave the state a reputation as a judicial "hellhole." Making matters worse was the state's rule of joint and several liability, under which a defendant that was as little as one percent at fault could be forced to pay up to half the total amount of damages. As a result, deep-pockets defendants, especially out-of-state corporations, were vulnerable to judgments that were far out of proportion to their wrongdoing.

Tort reformers warned that Mississippi's legal climate was harming the state's economy. Beginning in 2002, the legislature took steps to address the problem. House Bill 2 imposed a $500,000 cap on noneconomic damages in malpractice cases. House Bill 19 imposed limits on punitive damages in all civil cases; those limits ranged from 4 percent of net worth for defendants

## Trial lawyers use "junk science."

Tort reformers complain that judges have been too willing to admit "junk science" into evidence. Specialists in dubious fields such as "accidentology" have appeared in court, along with experts who advance theories, such as "chemical AIDS," that were rejected by mainstream scientists. Max Boot has argued that the lawyers who represent breast-implant plaintiffs relied heavily on faulty science:

worth less than 50 million dollars to 20 million dollars for defendants worth more than one billion dollars.

Two years later, lawmakers passed House Bill 13, a more comprehensive tort-reform measure that took effect September 1, 2004. It limits "forum shopping" by requiring a plaintiff to sue a corporate defendant where it has its principal place of business. If the defendant is out of state, the plaintiff must sue in the district where the tort occurred. If the tort occurred in Mississippi, the plaintiff must sue in her home district. The bill also discourages mass-tort cases by requiring each plaintiff in a multi-plaintiff lawsuit to prove that he or she had filed suit in the proper district.

House Bill 13 also lowered some of the 2002 limits on punitive damages, imposed a one-million-dollar cap on noneconomic damages in all civil cases, and tightened the malpractice cap by classifying disfigurement as "noneconomic" and eliminating language that would have eventually raised the cap to one million dollars. The bill also addressed the problem of joint and several liability. It limits an individual defendant's liability to the percentage to which it was at fault.

At the same time, Mississippi voters elected pro-tort reform justices to their state's supreme court. Those justices have tightened the standard for admitting expert testimony, and interpreted the court rules to make it more difficult for trial lawyers to turn individual lawsuits into mass-tort cases. Reformers believe that the new rules may result in the dismissal of tens of thousands of asbestos cases, most of which were filed by plaintiffs who lived in other states.

The judges allowed a traveling road show of "expert" testifiers into one courtroom after another, where they presented juries with just enough pseudoscientific mumbo jumbo to justify a verdict in favor of a sympathetic, sick plaintiff. . . . Many of these experts made hundreds of thousands of dollars a year from their courtroom activities. None had published a single peer-reviewed study in a reputable scientific journal backing up their claims.[69]

That evidence was ultimately discredited by mainstream scientists. In the meantime, however, defendants paid billions of dollars in damages.

> • **Should the judge, rather than the two sides' lawyers, be in charge of calling expert witnesses at trial?**

According to tort reformers, the worst abuses have occurred in asbestos cases. At one of President Bush's appearances in Michigan, his guest, Professor Lester Brickman of Yeshiva University Law School, commented on claims by plaintiffs who were not sick:

These are truly meritless claims. Nonetheless, they're supported by medical testimony from a handful of medical experts routinely selected by plaintiff lawyers who are not acting in good faith, in terms of supplying diagnosis, but are, in fact, responding to enormous financial incentives, which is to say, millions of dollars in fees that they generate for reading the X rays in the right way.

These meritless claims are also supported by the activities of screening companies hired by the plaintiff lawyers, who administer pulmonary function tests, which fail to adhere to medical standards, and produce false evidence of lung impairment. And finally, these meritless claims are supported by false witness testimony.[70]

The Manhattan Institute, which favors tort reform, has added that plaintiffs used junk science in lawsuits that involved Benedictin, an anti–morning sickness drug; Fen-Phen, a diet drug; and Norplant and IUDs. All of those products were approved by the FDA.

> • **Do you trust the FDA and other federal agencies? Are they putting the interests of corporations above those of the public?**

## Lawyers use lawsuits to extort and intimidate.

Tort reformers argue that today's rules of procedure, interpreted liberally by some judges, give baseless lawsuits an undeserved "settlement value." In other words, it is less risky for the defendant to settle, even if the merits weigh heavily in his or her favor, because of the possibility of a judgment large enough to bankrupt him or her. As the Hope Street Group, a group of business leaders, explained:

> The mere cost of litigation is not a barrier to frivolous suits with big settlement potential. For example, imagine a frivolous claim for $10,000,000 in damages with only a 1% probability of success. The expected settlement value of such a claim is still $100,000, well worth the time of a plaintiff's attorney who can extract that value quickly from a risk-averse defendant.[71]

Large companies are not the only targets of "junk" lawsuits. Victor Schwartz, the general counsel of the ATRA, explained that they plague small businesses as well:

> We're not talking about civil rights actions, but stuff not in the headlines—nickel and dime, $10,000, $15,000, $20,000 claims. They [small businesses] have no weaponry to fight them.
>
> This is the bottom of the barrel of the plaintiffs' bar. They bring a $20,000 claim against a restaurant owner for a person

who was never in the restaurant. The lawyer calls and tries to settle for just under the cost of the defense.[72]

Reformers also believe that trial lawyers abuse the rules that govern discovery. Although those rules were intended to make litigation less of a sport, trial lawyers have found ways to use the discovery process to play for time and make cases more expensive to defend. Some even use discovery to bully the defendant, along with those close to him or her, in an effort to make the suit so uncomfortable that he or she settles it. There are, in fact, few checks on abuse because discovery takes place outside the courtroom and without supervision by the judge.

> • **Should judges supervise discovery more closely? Are they doing enough to punish lawyers who abuse it?**

Finally, some plaintiffs use lawsuits to intimidate political opponents. The best-known of these suits are called "strategic lawsuits against public participation," or SLAPPs. The most common targets of SLAPPs are activists who mobilize community opposition to a proposed business expansion or property development. Most SLAPPs have little merit and are thrown out of court or dropped long before the trial. Nevertheless, they often accomplish their objective: Activists typically drop their campaigns rather than spend the time and money to fight the suit. Other plaintiffs have sued the news media, makers of documentaries, and creators of derogatory Websites in efforts to silence them. Critics warn that these lawsuits undermine the First Amendment:

> If independent-minded journalists cannot be outlawed they can be bankrupted. Until it was reduced and then thrown out in 1999, a $223 million libel verdict hung over the *Wall Street Journal*. The paper had published a hostile story that was right in its essence but wrong in some particulars. . . . Indeed, given where tort law has gone, the amendment would today

be worthless even in the U.S. if not for a 1964 Supreme Court decision, which threw out an Alabama jury's verdict against the *New York Times*.[73]

## Lawsuits reward irresponsible behavior.

Tort reformers point out that, until the middle of the twentieth century, the substantive law favored defendants and thus forced people to take responsibility for their own behavior. Today, however, it has become too easy for plaintiffs to use the legal system to shift the blame for their misfortunes, which are often self-inflicted. As *Newsweek* reporters Stuart Taylor and Evan Thomas observed, "Many Americans sue because they have come to believe that they have the 'right' to impose the costs and burdens of defending a lawsuit on anyone who angers them, regardless of fault or blame."[74] Max Boot cited several examples in which plaintiffs managed to force others to pay for their own actions:

- A New Hampshire woman who was bitten by her friend's pit bull sued her friend's landlord, arguing that the landlord was liable under state law for allowing dangerous conditions on its property. After a verdict in the woman's favor, the case was settled for 1.1 million dollars.

- A Chicago man was electrocuted when he relieved himself on some railroad tracks. Even though he was extremely intoxicated at the time and ignored a series of obstacles to get to the tracks, a jury awarded his widow 1.5 million dollars.

- A mugger was caught in the act and shot in the back by New York City police officers. After getting out of prison, the mugger sued the officers for using excessive force. The jury awarded him 4.3 million dollars.

The problem with those decisions, Boot said, is that "The courts are trying to provide a remedy for every conceivable 'victim,' and in the process, they hold no one accountable for his own conduct."[75]

## Summary

Today's liberal rules of procedure make it easy for plaintiffs to

## THE LETTER OF THE LAW

## Rule 11: Punishing Lawyers Who Abuse the System

Tort reformers believe that judges should make greater use of Rule 11 of the Federal Rules of Civil Procedure, which authorizes them to sanction, or impose penalties on, lawyers who abuse the system by filing unfounded lawsuits or frivolous pretrial motions. Rule 11 applies only in federal trials, but most states have court rules with at least some comparable provisions.

Rule 11(b) provides that, when a lawyer presents a pleading, motion, or other paper to the court, he or she is certifying that:

(1) He or she is not presenting it for an improper purpose, such as harassing the other side, unnecessary delaying the case, or making it more expensive.

(2) The arguments in the case are justified by existing law or by a non-frivolous argument that existing legal principles should be changed.

(3) The allegations are either supported by evidence or likely to be supported by evidence he or she will find later in the case.

(4) If he or she is denying the other side's allegations, either the evidence justifies the denial or he or she reasonably concludes those allegations are untrue.

Rule 11(c)(2) provides that allowable sanctions include a fine, an order to pay the other side's legal fees and costs of defending a frivolous motion, or "directives of a nonmonetary nature." A sanction for violating this rule must be limited to "what is sufficient to deter repetition of such conduct or comparable conduct by others similarly situated."

get their cases before juries and, once there, to use faulty science to prove their cases. The cost of defending even a weak case can be so high that many defendants settle rather than fight. There are few checks on baseless litigation: The losing party is not required to pay the other side's legal fees, and judges do little to punish lawyers who abuse the system. Some lawsuits are attempts to extort money from deep-pockets defendants or even to intimidate political opponents. Others are efforts by irresponsible people to blame others for their own actions.

---

In 2004, the House of Representatives passed H.R. 4571, which would have strengthened Rule 11 by requiring judges to impose sanctions for every violation. It also contained a "three strikes" rule under which a lawyer sanctioned three times by the same federal court would be suspended from practicing there for one year. The bill died in the Senate.

Some critics argued that it was unnecessary to make Rule 11 tougher. Georgene Vairo, a professor at Loyola Law School in Los Angeles, commented, "This is more about ideology and symbols. The rule is virtually as potent today as it used to be, not to mention that you have other tools out there, all sorts of things to sanction lawyers who are bad, and judges are now much more attuned to using those tools."[*] Others called the bill "tort reform through the back door," an attempt to use the rules of procedure to carry out reforms that died in Congress.

Some experts also believe that making Rule 11 sanctions mandatory would lead to more abuses of the justice system. The Judicial Conference of the United States warned that mandatory sanctions, which were in effect from 1983 to 1993,

> [were] abused by resourceful lawyers and an entire 'cottage industry' developed that churned tremendously wasteful satellite litigation that had everything to do with strategic gamesmanship and little to do with underlying claims. Rule 11 motions came to be met with counter motions that sought Rule 11 sanctions for making the original Rule 11 motion.[**]

[*] Marcia Coyle, "House Votes to Bring Bite Back to Rule 11," *National Law Journal*, September 27, 2004.

[**] Letter from the Judicial Conference of the United States to James Sensenbrenner, Jr., Chairman, House Judiciary Committee, July 9, 2004.

# Baseless Lawsuits Are the Exception, Not the Rule

Walt Shofner, a Texas businessman, sued a large computer-services firm that allegedly persuaded one of his clients to break a contract. The jury voted to award Shofner 8 million dollars in punitive damages. Texas's tort-reform law capped the punitive-damage award at $200,000. After the verdict, a disappointed Shofner said, "Tort reform assumes that all plaintiffs are crooks. But if a case gets far enough to get an award, that's not frivolous."[76]

Although many Americans assume that tort reform is aimed at "junk" and frivolous lawsuits, consumer advocates point out that some of its casualties are deserving plaintiffs like Shofner. Ralph Nader and Wesley Smith described the reformers' "bait and switch" strategy:

> Play on Americans' suspicions about greedy "shyster" lawyers, i.e., those lawyers who represent individuals seeking

Texas Governor Rick Perry, center, shakes hands with State Representative Joe Nixon during a ceremonial bill signing on June 11, 2003. The bill set damage award caps for pain and suffering in medical malpractice cases and created new protections for businesses against liability lawsuits.

compensation for personal injuries. Take the few lawsuits each year where juries award large punitive damages and distort the facts beyond recognition. Spread fears of job loss, of high insurance premiums caused by lawsuits, and of a national economy crippled by a litigation "explosion."[77]

## Frivolous lawsuits are rare.

Despite tort reformers' complaints, few truly frivolous suits— for example, suing the referees for a bad call in a football game—are actually filed by individuals. That is because the civil justice system provides little incentive to file them. Frivolous suits rarely succeed; therefore, a plaintiff's lawyer, who typically works on a contingent-fee basis, will end up with little or nothing in return for the investment of time and money in the case.

There are other reasons not to file such lawsuits. As Nader and Smith pointed out:

> Where frivolous and phony lawsuits are filed, there are sufficient checks and balances in the legal system to ensure that the vast majority of such claims are defeated, soundly and promptly. . . . If a plaintiff has no solid legal claim or can offer no facts to fully support a claim, the judge can dismiss the case on the defendant's motion before any trial.[78]

One check is Rule 11 of the Federal Rules of Civil Procedure, which allows a judge to fine lawyers who file abusive pleadings. Other rules, which the Supreme Court has interpreted favorably for defendants, give judges broad powers to act as "gatekeepers," further reducing the chances that a weak case will go to trial or that junk science will be presented to the jury. Finally, a lawyer's sense of duty toward the client and profession and the possibility that he or she will gain a reputation for incompetence are further checks on baseless suits.

## Most frivolous lawsuits are filed by businesses.

Trial lawyers argue that tort-reform measures focus on a small fraction of lawsuits—those filed by individuals against corporations. They also claim that corporate defendants are capable of defending themselves: They have the means to hire the best lawyers and experts and, if necessary, to fight a drawn-out battle. Furthermore, corporations are "repeat players" that are familiar with the courts, whereas most victims of corporate misconduct have not been in the system before.

• **Do the news media pay too much attention to abusive suits by plaintiffs and not enough attention to abusive suits by businesses?**

Nor are corporations reluctant to sue: By one estimate, nearly half of all civil lawsuits are disputes between corporations. According to former insurance company executive J. Russell Tyldesley, "[c]orporations with revenues of $1 billion or more have an average of 86 lawsuits pending at any given time. Most of this litigation is employment/labor disputes, contract disputes and intellectual property cases."[79] Some of those suits are baseless. According to Joshua Green, a senior editor at *The Atlantic*, "The single factor most clogging the judicial system is frivolous litigation brought by corporations against corporations, which don't involve independent trial lawyers at all."[80] The Foundation for Taxpayer and Consumer Rights agrees. In 2004, it listed the top five cases of "corporate lawsuit abuse." The offenders included Allstate Insurance, which sued Kellogg's, alleging that flammable Pop-Tarts were the cause of a fire in the home of one of its policyholders; Caterpillar, Inc., which sued the Walt Disney Company for portraying bulldozers in a bad light in the film *George of the Jungle 2*; Mattel, Inc., which sued an artist who exhibited photos of a Barbie doll in poses that allegedly defamed her character; Kellogg's, which claimed that its "Toucan Sam" logo for Froot Loops cereal would be damaged by Toucan Golf's golf-playing bird; and Procter and Gamble, which sued Amway Corporation for allegedly spreading rumors that its "moon and stars" logo had Satanic connotations. Consumer advocates argue that those cases are more representative of the true problem of frivolous lawsuits.

## Corporate defendants abuse the civil justice system.

Critics argue that tort reform does not stop defendants from waging "wars of attrition." They accuse corporations and the law firms that represent them of using delaying tactics, such as raising frivolous objections to requests for information, refusing to turn over material, and narrowly interpreting what the plaintiff requested. Nader and Smith explained:

> The strategy is to avoid disclosing the truth or at least delay doing so as long as possible so that the truth, when it comes out at all, is dribbled in such a way that it can't be put together coherently for trial. You end up running out of time or judicial patience and having to go to trial without the evidence

# FROM THE BENCH

## Are Damage Caps Fair? *Maurin* v. *Hall*

For Joseph and Yvette Maurin, the death of their five-year-old daughter, Shay, was not just a tragedy. It was the beginning of a frustrating legal battle in the Wisconsin courts.

The Maurins sued Shay's doctor, Gordon Hall, alleging that he had committed malpractice by not diagnosing her life-threatening condition in time to save her. Their suit consisted of two claims for damages. One claim was for Shay's pain and suffering; when Shay died, her parents "inherited" it. The other claim was based on their loss of Shay's companionship.

The jury awarded the Maurins $550,000 for Shay's pain and suffering and 2.5 million dollars for the loss of her companionship. The entire award consisted of noneconomic damages. The state of Wisconsin, however, capped noneconomic damages in "wrongful death" cases—those in which the victim of wrongdoing died—at $150,000 and capped damages at $350,000 in malpractice cases. The Maurins argued that the wrongful-death cap was unconstitutional, and the trial judge agreed with them.

Dr. Hall appealed. He argued that damage caps were constitutional and that they applied in this case because all the damages were noneconomic. His appeal reached the Supreme Court of Wisconsin. In *Maurin* v. *Hall*, 274 Wis. 2d 28, 682 N.W.2d 866 (2004), a 4–3 majority ruled that the Maurins could recover only $150,000.

Justice David Prosser wrote the majority opinion. Because Dr. Hall's malpractice caused Shay's death, he reasoned that the Maurins' malpractice case had become you're entitled to. Then, in the next case, you start the effort all over again.[81]

Some also contend that paying defense lawyers by the hour creates a greater incentive to abuse the system than paying trial lawyers a percentage of the client's recovery. Trial lawyer Elihu Inselbuch explained:

> Since the attorney's fee is contingent upon success, the attorney has a compelling economic incentive not to accept cases

a wrongful-death case, which meant that the $150,000 cap applied. He also concluded that the cap applied to the Maurins' entire suit, even though it consisted of two claims. He pointed out that state lawmakers had "shown a consistent pattern of funneling and restricting medical malpractice actions to control costs," including placing caps on noneconomic damages. Justice Prosser rejected the Maurins' argument that the $150,000 cap was unconstitutional. He also rejected their argument that the cap deprived them of trial by jury, pointing out that a jury still determined liability and assessed damages.

Chief Justice Shirley Abrahamson sharply criticized the majority's reasoning, writing: "Forgetting the victims of malpractice, the majority errs in its interpretation because its total and sole concern is for health care providers and the cost of insurance premiums. The majority cynically attributes this attitude to the legislature and the strength of the health care providers' lobby." The law, as she read it, provided the Maurins with one claim for Shay's pain and suffering and another for the loss of her companionship. Abrahamson did not consider all damage caps unconstitutional, but she argued that the majority opinion left the Maurins with so small a recovery that it deprived them of trial by jury and a legal remedy for the damages they suffered. She added that the cap on damages was unconstitutional for another reason: It treated malpractice victims less favorably than other victims of wrongdoing, thus depriving them of equal protection of the law.

in which the probability of success is so low as to make the case a poor investment of time and money. . . .

If any group of lawyers has an incentive by reason of their fee arrangements for delay or for taking frivolous positions in litigation, it is counsel who bill by the hour.[82]

Corporations have other incentives to prolong litigation. Most can deduct litigation expenses against their income for tax purposes and treat judgments as a cost of doing business and pass it on to consumers. In addition, in most states, a plaintiff's claim does not start earning interest until the court enters judgment; thus, the longer it takes to settle a case, the cheaper it is for the defendant.

> • **Do corporations cover up their wrongdoing? Is enough being done to stop it?**

Trial lawyers also accuse corporations of using the justice system to hide their wrongdoing. One common tactic is to ask the court for a protective order, which keeps others from finding out what the corporation turned over during discovery. Protective orders not only minimize bad publicity, but also prevent trial lawyers from sharing information—even though defense lawyers remain free to do so. Another tactic is to insist that the settlement be kept confidential; as a result, the media do not learn the amount and, more important, other trial lawyers suing the same corporation have to guess what their case is worth. Finally, some corporations that lose at trial threaten to appeal unless the plaintiff agrees to a settlement that takes the case out of the public record, effectively treating the lawsuit as though it never happened. That prevents other trial lawyers from using the judgment against it in future cases that involve the same facts.

## The real crisis involves insurance, not lawsuits.

It has been argued that the "litigation crisis," especially in the area of malpractice, was created by the insurance industry.

According to the Council of State Governments, "Many of the problems of the medical malpractice insurance industry are related to the health care field and the market structure of the insurance industry. Tort reform [which began in the late 1970s] did not address these aspects, so it didn't make lasting changes to the system."[83]

The insurance industry is cyclical. When the stock market is strong, companies earn a generous return on their investments; some try to attract money to invest by lowering premiums and even insuring those who are bad risks. When the stock market is weak, insurance companies are forced to make up the difference by raising premiums. Many believe that the current crisis began in 2000, when the stock market "bubble" burst, and continued when the economy slumped after the September 11, 2001, terrorist attacks.

> • **Are insurance companies' profits too high? Should they be regulated by law?**

Consumer advocates cite Texas as an example. In 2003, state lawmakers imposed a $250,000 cap on noneconomic damages, in part because insurance companies argued that a cap was needed to hold down costs. The following year, GE Medical Protective, the nation's largest malpractice insurer, asked the Texas Department of Insurance for permission to raise premiums by 19 percent. In its filing, the company claimed that the damage cap would reduce its losses by only one percent. Many consumer advocates believe that California's approach to insurance costs is more effective. In 1988, voters approved Proposition 103, which requires a public hearing on a proposed premium increase. The Foundation for Taxpayer and Consumer Rights has argued that the measure has saved California policyholders 23 billion dollars.

## Tort reformers have a hidden agenda.

Trial lawyers accuse tort reformers of using deceptive phrases such as "junk science" and "tort tax" to hide their real agenda of

*(continued on page 96)*

## Statistics on State Tort Cases, 2001

The federal Bureau of Justice Statistics studied 7,948 tort trials that took place in the nation's 75 largest counties during 2001. The following are major findings of the study.

- The largest category of cases involved traffic crashes (36 percent); that was followed by dangerous premises (11 percent).

- Plaintiffs won 52 percent of trials. They won more often in nonjury trials (65 percent) than in jury trials (51 percent).

- Plaintiffs were most likely to win cases that involved animal attacks (67 percent), traffic crashes (61 percent), and exposure to asbestos (60 percent). They won only 27 percent of malpractice cases.

- The median award was $27,000. The median was slightly higher in jury trials ($28,000) than in nonjury trials ($23,000). Awards of one million dollars or more were more common in jury trials (7.8 percent) than nonjury trials (5.4 percent).

- The highest median award, about 1.7 million dollars, came in asbestos cases. There were only 19 such cases. In addition, asbestos cases involved an average of 3.2 plaintiffs, compared to 1.4 in tort cases in general.

- The median award in malpractice cases was $422,000. Slightly less than 30 percent of awards were for one million dollars or more.

- A total of 442 cases alleged wrongful death; 65 percent of them involved malpractice. Plaintiffs won 36 percent of those cases, and the median award was $961,000.

- Punitive-damage awards totaled 367.1 million dollars, or about 16 percent of all damages awarded.

- Punitive damages were awarded in 217 cases, or 2.7 percent of the total. Forty-five cases resulted in awards larger than $250,000 and 23 in awards larger than one million dollars.

- Cases that involved libel or slander were most likely (59 percent) to result in a punitive-damage award; they were followed by cases that involved intentional torts (36 percent) and false arrest or imprisonment (26 percent).

- In 40 percent of the cases where punitive damages were awarded, the punitive award was larger than the compensatory award. In 18 percent of those cases, the punitive award was more than four times compensatory damages, the Supreme Court's current yardstick for an "excessive" award.

- The largest damage award—90 million dollars in compensatory damages and 364.5 million dollars in punitive damages, later reduced to 121 million dollars—occurred in a business dispute, not a tort case.

- Only one case could be classified as a class action, and it was not a tort case. It was an action by 2,400 insurance claims adjusters to recover overtime pay.

The study also compared 2001 results with those from 1992. The findings included these:

- Tort cases fell by 32 percent, with the largest percentage decreases in product-liability and dangerous-premises cases.

- Plaintiffs were slightly more successful in 2001 than 1992, when they won 47 percent of the time.

- The median jury award in 1992 was $64,000. Adjusting for inflation, the median award fell by 56 percent between 1992 and 2001.

- Between 1992 and 2001, the median award rose by 288 percent in product-liability cases and by 70 percent in malpractice cases. Product cases accounted for only 1.3 percent and malpractice cases for only 9.7 percent of all tort cases in 2001.

Source: Bureau of Justice Statistics, *Civil Trial Cases and Verdicts in Large Counties, 2001.* Washington, D.C.: Bureau of Justice Statistics, 2004. Available at *http://www.ojp.usdoj.gov/ bjs/pub/pdf/ctcvlc01.pdf.*

*(continued from page 93)*

maximizing corporate profits. As Jamie Court, the president of the Foundation for Taxpayer and Consumer Rights, observed, "The only reason reforming corporations' frivolous litigation practices is not on the table on Capitol Hill is because big business is the unofficial sponsor of 'lawsuit abuse week' and of similar propaganda aimed at limiting the ability of injured individuals to hold big corporations accountable." [84] Reformers often portray themselves as friends of taxpayers and consumers, but they actually are a "who's who" of special interests—including chemical and pharmaceutical companies and manufacturers of guns, alcoholic beverages, and cigarettes—that have good reason to fear lawsuits.

## Factors That Affect Future Tort Costs

Tillinghast–Towers Perrin's 2004 update on tort costs identified seven factors that, in its opinion, will influence future costs:

1. Will auto liability claims continue their steady to slightly lower trend?

2. Will insurance companies have to set aside even more money to pay asbestos claims?

3. Will recent scandals involving mutual fund and brokerage companies generate significant tort costs?

4. Will damage caps and other reforms slow the growth of malpractice-related costs?

5. Have lawsuits against corporate directors and officers peaked?

6. Will obesity-related lawsuits start to generate significant costs?

7. Will lawsuits significantly increase the liability of prescription drug makers?

Source: Tillinghast–Towers Perrin, *U.S. Tort Costs: 2004 Update. Trends and Findings on the Costs of the U.S. Tort System*. New York: Tillinghast–Towers Perrin, 2004, p. 11. Available at *http://www.towersperrin.com/tillinghast/publications/reports/Tort_2004/Tort.pdf*.

Some believe that tort reform is motivated by party politics. In Texas, for example, Republican strategists used the issue to attract contributions from large corporations and to help fund their party's candidates, including those running for the state supreme court. Some Democrats argue that tort reform is part of an effort to weaken their party by cutting off its trial-lawyer supporters' source of income. It has even been suggested that some reformers are hiding behind a popular cause—curtailing lawsuit abuse—but their real objective is to roll back laws that protect women, minorities, and people with disabilities.

- **Do you favor a ban on corporate contributions to political parties and candidates?**

## Summary

Despite reformers' claims that "junk" lawsuits are a serious problem, trial lawyers rarely file such suits because they have little to gain by doing so. In fact, corporations file the majority of frivolous suits, yet they are not the target of tort reformers. In addition, corporate defendants engage in abusive practices such as prolonging litigation and insisting on settlements that keep their wrongdoing secret. The strongest supporters of the tort-reform movement are corporations and insurance companies. They are taking advantage of popular resentment of lawyers and lawsuits to maximize their profits and make themselves less accountable.

# The Future of Tort Reform

The 2004 election gave tort reformers reason to be optimistic. Voters reelected President Bush, an outspoken advocate of reform measures, and Republicans increased their majority in Congress. At the state level, voters approved most of the tort-reform proposals on the ballot and defeated most state supreme court candidates who were backed by trial lawyers. In addition, opinion polls show strong support for tort reform. Eighty-six percent of Americans backed limits on trial lawyers' fees, 73 percent wanted lawyers who filed frivolous suits to be penalized, and 63 percent favored a cap on noneconomic damages in malpractice cases.

## Proposals for Reform
### In Congress

During President Bush's first term, Congress passed a number of small-scale tort-reform measures, including restrictions on suits against airplane manufacturers, drug companies, teachers, and makers of antiterrorism devices.

After the 2004 election, the ATRA predicted that three major pieces of legislation would pass during the president's second term:

(1) Class-action reform: The Class Action Fairness Act of 2005 became law in February 2005. It allows defendants to move large, interstate class-action cases from state court to federal court, makes it harder for defendants to pay plaintiffs in coupons rather than cash, and bans settlements that favor some plaintiffs at the expense of others. Reformers believe that the act will prevent "forum shopping" and put large class-action suits in the hands of federal judges who are better qualified to handle them. Consumer advocates warn, however, that federal courts will be less sympathetic to class members than state court judges, especially in consumer-protection and employees'-rights cases, and some fear that moving class actions to federal court erodes states' rights.

(2) Asbestos legislation: The 108th Congress considered a bill that would have moved asbestos suits from the courts to a federal agency, established procedures for evaluating and paying claims, and created a fund from which victims would be paid.[86] It died because lawmakers could not agree on the size of the fund. Supporters maintain that Congress must act because asbestos filings continue to increase (there were more than 100,000 in 2003 alone) and that the caseload is clogging court dockets and delaying payment to the sick and dying. They add that the majority of suits—90 percent by one estimate—are

filed by plaintiffs who are not sick, and courts are not screening out baseless claims.

(3) Malpractice reform: The AMA supports a nationwide $250,000 cap on noneconomic damages. A bill in the 108th Congress would have imposed such a cap.[87] Supporters argue that noneconomic damages drive up the cost of health care and are not awarded on a consistent and objective basis. Some even contend that compensation for pain and suffering is an ill-advised experiment that should be ended. Phil Hinderberger, an executive at Norcal Mutual Insurance Company, remarked, "A soldier injured in combat is not entitled to any pain and suffering. A worker injured in the workplace is not entitled to any pain and suffering."[88] Opponents of caps maintain that they unfairly deny deserving victims a remedy, infringe on the right to trial by jury, and discriminate against the poor.

Also on reformers' agenda is a "three strikes" rule,[89] under which a lawyer fined three times by the same court for filing abusive pleadings would be barred from that court for one year; the so-called "cheeseburger bill,"[90] which would bar obesity-related suits against the food industry; and a ban on lawsuits against manufacturers and sellers of guns.[91]

> • **Which should take the lead in tort reform, Congress or the states?**

## In the States

Reform measures at the state level include these:

- Limits on damages: A majority of states have capped noneconomic damages in malpractice suits, and most states' appeals courts have found them constitutional. Some states may extend caps to civil suits other than malpractice cases. In 2003, for example, Texas voters approved a constitutional amendment that gave the legislature the authority to do so. Punitive damages are another target of reformers. Many states have established a stricter burden of proof. In Texas, punitive damages may be awarded "only if the claimant proves by clear and convincing evidence that the harm with respect to which the claimant seeks recovery of [punitive] damages results from: (1) fraud; (2) malice; or (3) gross negligence."[92] Other proposals would cap punitive-damage awards; ban multiple awards for the same incident; require that awards be paid to the state, not to the plaintiff; and forbid juries to consider the defendant's misconduct in other states. Reformers argue that punitive-damage awards are out of proportion to the defendant's wrongdoing and represent a windfall for plaintiffs and their lawyers. Opponents warn that caps will result in punitive damages becoming another cost of doing business and thus encourage unsafe products and practices.

- Restricting joint and several liability: Most states have either abolished or restricted the rule of joint and several liability. Those who favor this reform argue that it is unfair to force a defendant to pay for others' misconduct simply because it has deeper pockets. Opponents argue that it is less unfair to force a wealthy defendant to pay other defendants' share of the judgment than for victims to receive little or no compensation.

- Other malpractice-related reforms: Some states require the plaintiff's lawyer to submit a malpractice suit to a medical review panel before filing it. Other reforms include minimum qualifications for expert witnesses, protection for doctors who disclose to patients the risks associated with medical procedures, and requiring that judgments be paid in installments rather than as a lump sum.

## Tort Reform at the Ballot Box

In the 2004 election, voters in a record number of states faced ballot questions relating to tort reform. Proposals in four states—Florida, Nevada, Oregon, and Wyoming—dealt with medical malpractice. The AMA labeled all of them "crisis" states, where doctors were moving out or scaling back their practices because they could not afford liability insurance. Trial lawyers countered that the ballot proposals would give the medical profession undeserved special treatment. As Bill Bradley of the Nevada Trial Lawyers Association remarked, "All that those limitations do is make it impossible for victims to hire lawyers as good as the lawyers the doctors and hospitals can hire."

Florida voters approved a constitutional amendment that limited contingent fees to 30 percent of the first $250,000 in damages and 10 percent of the amount more than $250,000. Doctors suffered a couple of setbacks at the polls, however. Voters approved a measure that would allow patients to see medical records. Doctors worry that confidential documents used in quality-control programs could find their way into court. They also approved a "three strikes" law that would bar a doctor from practicing in Florida after three malpractice judgments against him.

In Nevada, voters approved a cap on noneconomic damages. Trial lawyers are expected to challenge its constitutionality. Voters also rejected two trial lawyer–backed proposals. One, labeled a restriction on frivolous lawsuits, actually would have made it harder to penalize lawyers who filed baseless suits. The other would have banned limits on contingent fees and damage awards.

Caps on damages narrowly lost in Oregon and Wyoming. Oregon doctors, however, view the cap as just one piece of the malpractice-liability puzzle. They

Pennsylvania has taken steps to eliminate the "culture of blame" in health care by requiring health-care facilities to report serious medical errors to the state on a confidential basis.

- "Loser pays" rule: Some reformers believe that American courts should follow the lead of other Western countries and require the losing party in a

plan to lobby the legislature for reforms such as an excess liability fund, tighter restrictions on expert witnesses, and payment of large awards in installments rather than as a lump sum.

Elsewhere in the country, other reforms were approved by voters:

- Californians voted to rein in lawyers who act as "private attorneys general." They approved an amendment to the state's unfair business practices law to bar a lawyer from suing unless he or she has an actual client who was in fact injured. Only the attorney general and local law-enforcement officials may enforce the law on behalf of the public.

- Trial lawyers suffered setbacks in judicial elections. In the most expensive judicial race in American history, Republican Lloyd Karmeier defeated Democratic Appeals Court Judge Gordon Maag for a seat on the Illinois Supreme Court. Maag, who is from Madison County—one of the nation's most pro-plaintiff jurisdictions—also lost his Appeals Court seat in a retention election, the first time that happened in 40 years. In Mississippi, three of four trial lawyer–backed candidates for the state supreme court lost; the fourth, an incumbent, won in a runoff election. In Ohio, where the legislature and judiciary have waged a running battle over tort reform, three supreme court candidates who had received large trial lawyer contributions were defeated. In West Virginia, a supreme court justice whose decisions favored trial lawyers lost his bid for reelection.

lawsuit to pay the other side's legal fees. They believe that the so-called "English rule" would discourage baseless lawsuits and, at the same time, give lawyers an incentive to represent clients with small but valid claims. Opponents argue that the rule would fall most heavily on debtors, who could end up paying twice for the same claim. Others contend that its effects would go beyond tort cases. Former federal appeals court judge Abner Mikva asserted, "If the English rule had been in effect here, none of the civil rights cases would have been brought. If they had lost, a single lawsuit would have wiped out their treasuries."[93]

- Immunities: Some states' laws bar or restrict certain types of lawsuits, such as those against gun makers, fast-food chains, or manufacturers of FDA-approved products. Supporters of immunities argue that they protect vulnerable industries, promote consumer choice, and encourage personal responsibility. Opponents argue that immunities leave innocent victims and their families without compensation. In addition, as the Center for Justice and Democracy has argued, "Any industry with money or clout lines up every year to get their own special laws ensuring they are never held responsible for what they do wrong."[94]

- **Should there be a special federal court to hear all mass-tort and class-action cases?**

## Alternatives to Litigation
### Alternative Dispute Resolution

There are several means by which parties can resolve disputes without going to trial. One form of alternative dispute resolution

Florida Governor Jeb Bush speaks at a tort reform rally in Tallahassee, March 15, 2005. Florida was one of four states labeled "crisis" states by the American Medical Association, because Florida doctors had been moving out or scaling back their practices when they could no longer afford liability insurance.

(ADR) is mediation, in which the parties agree to meet with a third party to discuss a possible resolution of their dispute. The mediator's recommendation is not binding. Another approach, required by many states' rules of civil procedure, is some form of mandatory procedure aimed at encouraging settlement. In some states, a party who ignores a settlement recommendation and goes to trial faces financial penalties if he or she fails to win a better verdict at the trial.

A third form of ADR is arbitration, which is based on the parties' agreement to take their dispute before a neutral arbitrator rather than go to court. The arbitrator's decision is

## FROM THE BENCH

## Mandatory Arbitration of Disputes:
### *Borowiec* v. *Gateway 2000, Inc.*

Michael Borowiec, the buyer of a computer, filed suit against Gateway 2000, Inc. He argued that Gateway failed to repair his computer and therefore violated the federal Magnuson-Moss Warranty-Federal Trade Commission Improvement Act, as well as Illinois law.

Gateway asked the court to dismiss Borowiec's lawsuit. It argued that a clause in the standard warranty that accompanied his computer required disputes to be resolved by arbitration. The Circuit Court and Appellate Court of Illinois rejected Gateway's argument, concluding that the Magnuson-Moss Act barred a manufacturer from requiring a consumer to arbitrate a defective-product dispute. Gateway appealed to the Supreme Court of Illinois which, in *Borowiec* v. *Gateway 2000, Inc.*, 209 Ill. 2d 376, 808 N.E.2d 957 (2004), voted 5–2 to reverse the lower courts' decisions.

Justice Charles Freeman wrote the majority opinion. He concluded that Gateway's arbitration clause should be enforced. He observed that it was governed by the Federal Arbitration Act, a 1925 law that provides that an agreement to arbitrate cut off the parties' right to sue unless another act of Congress created such a right. He then concluded that the Magnuson-Moss Act had no effect on mandatory arbitration. Although it referred to a manufacturer's "informal dispute-resolution procedure," it envisioned such a procedure as a means of resolving a dispute *before* it went to court. Arbitration, on the other hand, was a means of resolving a dispute *without* going to court, and Magnuson-Moss never mentioned it. Justice Freeman added that an agreement to arbitrate did not take away a consumer's rights; it only provided that his dispute with the manufacturer would be heard in a forum other than a court of law.

final. Supporters believe that arbitration saves time and money because the rules are less formal and that it is fairer because arbitrators are more likely than juries to decide the dispute on the facts. Opponents contend that arbitrators favor corporations, which often select and pay for the arbitration firm and are familiar with the procedure. They add that arbitration denies plaintiffs important rights such as trial by jury and remedies such

Justice Thomas Kilbride dissented. In his view, Congress intended to create an exception to the Federal Arbitration Act. He pointed out that, in 1975, when it passed the Magnuson-Moss Act, arbitration was less sophisticated; he therefore read the term "informal dispute resolution" as referring to arbitration. In his view, Congress sought to encourage mechanisms for settling disputes out of court but also intended to preserve the consumer's right to sue if he or she was dissatisfied with the mechanism's decision. Justice Kilbride accused the majority of undermining that intent "by permitting manufacturers to slip mandatory, binding arbitration provisions into nonnegotiable consumer product warranties and, thus, to limit consumers' avenues of relief in the event of a warranty dispute." He added that corporations such as Gateway forced arbitration clauses on consumers who had no power to negotiate them.

Justice Philip Rarick also dissented. He agreed that the intent of the Magnuson-Moss Act was to bar mandatory arbitration of warranty disputes. He also warned that the majority's interpretation would give manufacturers an incentive to offer consumers nothing more favorable than arbitration, thus making Magnuson-Moss's informal dispute-resolution process meaningless. Although Justice Rarick conceded that arbitration was beneficial because it was cheaper and more flexible, he found that a blanket arbitration policy like Gateway's benefited the manufacturer at the consumer's expense. He observed, "If binding arbitration were advantageous to consumers, one would expect to find instances where warrantors were asking for judicial relief while consumers demanded arbitration. In fact, the reported decisions seem to be uniformly to the contrary."

as punitive and noneconomic damages. Furthermore, arbitration is often forced on consumers on a "take it or leave it" basis, for example, as part of a manufacturer's standard product warranty. Jeffrey White fears that consumers will, increasingly, be forced to sign away important rights:

> Even a low-wattage crystal ball can foretell a not-too-distant future when an automaker, pharmaceutical company, or any product seller will include a notice stating that by using the product, the consumer agrees to submit any products liability claim to an arbitration procedure set up by the manufacturer. Hotels may present such forms to their guests to cover injuries or even criminal attacks.[95]

### *"Medical Courts"*

A number of states are considering the creation of special "medical courts" to decide malpractice claims. These courts would have no juries; they instead would be presided over by a judge with medical expertise. They probably would be similar to state worker's compensation systems, where fault is not an issue and compensation is limited to economic damages. Supporters argue that claims that allege medical errors should not be decided by lay jurors. As William Sullivan, an Illinois physician, remarked, "I'm sure a lot of people would love to have some sympathetic jurors in a tax court. That's why they have tax courts—there's a bunch of specialized knowledge that you need, and it brings out a fairer verdict for both sides."[96] Other supporters point out that medical courts would provide more compensation to patients and less to lawyers. Opponents contend that medical courts would be biased in favor of doctors and that their awards would neither fully compensate victims nor discourage practices that lead to medical errors.

- **Should users of cigarettes and alcohol be forbidden to sue for injuries resulting from them?**

## Summary

Tort reformers believe that courts must reduce the scope of defendants' liability in order to avoid economic decline, just as nineteenth-century courts shifted to a fault-based standard in an effort to protect emerging industries. Defenders of the current system reply that the tort-reform movement is an overreaction or, even worse, an attempt to enrich large corporations at the expense of average Americans. In the years to come, the proposals likely to generate the most debate include malpractice and class-action reform, limits on noneconomic and punitive damages, and a legislative solution to asbestos litigation.

## Introduction

1 Philip. K. Howard, *The Death of Common Sense: How Law is Suffocating America.* New York: Random House, 1994, pp. 24–25.

2 Bryan A. Garner, ed. *Black's Law Dictionary.* St. Paul, MN: West Group, 2004, p. 1526.

3 *Brown* v. *Kendall,* 60 Mass. 292, 296 (1850).

4 *Pike* v. *Honsinger,* 155 N.Y. 201, 209, 49 N.E. 760, 762 (1898).

5 *Greenman* v. *Yuba Power Products,* 59 Cal. 2d 57, 62, 377 P.2d 897, 900 (1963)

6 Jay M. Feinman, "Torts," *The Oxford Companion to American Law.* New York: Oxford University Press, 2002, pp. 806–807.

7 98 Eng. Rep. 489 (C.P. 1763).

8 Jay M. Feinman, *Law 101: Everything You Need to Know About the American Legal System.* New York: Oxford University Press, 2000, p. 169.

## Overview

9 U.S. Const. amend. XIV, §1.

10 Feinman, *Law 101,* p. 93.

11 Ralph Nader and Wesley J. Smith, *No Contest: Corporate Lawyers and the Perversion of Justice in America.* New York: Random House, 1996, p. 309.

12 *World-Wide Volkswagen Corporation* v. *Woodson,* 444 U.S. 286, 291 (1980).

13 Mich. Comp. Laws Ann. §600.2591(3)(a).

14 Walter K. Olson, *The Rule of Lawyers: How the New Litigation Elite Threatens America's Rule of Law.* New York: St. Martin's Press, 2003, p. 248.

15 *United States* v. *Procter & Gamble Company,* 356 U.S. 677, 682 (1958).

16 Nader and Smith, *No Contest,* p. 63.

17 U.S. Const. amend. VII.

18 Howard, *Death of Common Sense,* p. 52.

## Point: America Is Experiencing a "Litigation Explosion"

19 Walter K. Olson, *The Litigation Explosion: What Happened When America Unleashed the Lawsuit.* New York: Penguin, 1991, p. 254.

20 Robert R. Gasaway, "The Problem of Tort Reform: Federalism and the Regulation of Lawyers," 25 Harvard J Law Publ P 3, Summer 2002, 953.

21 Paul Taubman. "Gross domestic product (GDP)." World Book Online Reference Center. 2005. World Book, Inc. April 5, 2005.

Available at *http://www.worldbankonline.com/ wb/Article?id=arr237330.*

22 Feinman, *Law 101,* p. 138.

23 Sheri Hall, "Malpractice Rates Drive Off Doctors," *Detroit News,* October 25, 2004.

24 "President Discusses Medical Liability Reform," Collinsville, Illinois, January 5, 2005. Available at *http://www.whitehouse.gov/ news/releases/2005/01/print/20050105-4 .html.*

25 N.Y. Gen. Bus. Law §349(h).

26 Feinman, *Law 101,* p. 111.

27 Stephen Moore. "Trial Lawyers on Trial." Published by Scripps-Howard News Service, May 2, 2003. Available at *http://www.clubfor-growth.org/scrippshoward/030502.php.*

28 Max Boot, *Out of Order: Arrogance, Corruption, and Incompetence on the Bench.* New York: Basic Books, 1998, p. 148.

## Counterpoint: Litigation Is Not a Serious Problem

29 Stephanie Mencimer, "False Alarm: How the Media Helps the Insurance Industry and the GOP Promote the Myth of America's 'Lawsuit Crisis,'" *Washington Monthly,* October 2004, p. 18.

30 Ibid.

31 David S. Clark, "Litigiousness," *The Oxford Companion to American Law,* p. 534.

32 Cal. Civ. Code §3333.2.

33 Fed. R. Evid. 702.

34 Americans for Insurance Reform. News Release; "Tillinghast's 'Tort Cost' Figures Vastly Overstate the Cost of American Legal System." Washington, DC: Americans for Insurance Reform, 2004, p. 1. Available at *http://www.insurance-reform.org/pr/ Tillinghast_Overstates.pdf.*

35 David G. Savage, "Trial Lawyers an Issue in Presidential Campaign," *Los Angeles Times,* October 10, 2004.

36 Joseph T. Hallinan, "In Malpractice Trials, Juries Rarely Have the Last Word," *Wall Street Journal,* November 30, 2004.

37 Jonathan D. Glater, "Study Disputes View of Costly Surge in Class-Action Suits," *New York Times,* January 14, 2004.

38 Dan Zegart, "The Right Wing's Drive for 'Tort Reform,'" *The Nation,* October 25, 2004.

39 Feinman, Jay M. 2000, *Law 101: Everything You Need to Know About the American Legal*

*System*, New York, NY: Oxford University Press, p. 154-155.

40  Quintin Johnson and Dan W. Hopson. 1967. *Lawyers and Their Work: an Analysis of the Legal Profession in the United States and England*. Indianapolis: Bobbs-Merrill, 1967

41  Jon Robins, "A Very Uncivil War," TheLawyer.com (UK), November 22, 2004. Available at *http://www.thelawyer.com/ cgi-bin/item.cgi?id=112966&d=11&h= 24&f=23*.

## Point: Lawsuits Are Unfair to Both Businesses and Consumers

42  Olson, *Rule of Lawyers*, p. 7.

43  Manhattan Institute, *Trial Lawyers, Inc.: A Report on the Lawsuit Industry in America 2003*. New York: Manhattan Institute, Center for Legal Policy, 2003, p. 9. Available at *http://www.manhattan-institute.org/ triallawyersinc.pdf*.

44  Howard, "History of American Law," *The Oxford Companion to American Law*, p. 396.

45  Stuart Taylor, Jr., and Even Thomas, "Civil Wars," *Newsweek*, December 15, 2003.

46  Olson, *Litigation Explosion*, p. 195.

47  Hope Street Group, *Just Compensation: Restoring Fairness and Efficiency to America's Civil Justice System*. Arlington, VA: Hope Street Group, 2004, p. 3. Available at *http://www.hopestreetgroup.org/publica- tions/Tort%20Reform.pdf*.

48  Michael Barone, "Re-examining Tort Law," *U.S. News & World Report* online column, August 30, 2002. Available at *http://www.usnews.com/usnews/opinion/ baroneweb/mb_020830.htm*.

49  Manhattan Institute, *Trial Lawyers, Inc.* p. 8.

50  Ibid., p. 17.

51  Rodd Zolkos, "Jurists Urge Industry Involve- ment," *Business Insurance*, February 16, 2004.

52  Martin J. Hatlie and Susan E. Sheridan, "The Medical Liability Crisis of 2003: Must We Squander the Chance to Put Patients First," *Health Affairs* 22 (2003):37.

53  Tillinghast-Towers Perrin. 2003. *Trends and Findings on the Costs of the U.S. Tort System*, 1-2. New York, NY: Tillinghast-Towers Perrin. Available online at *http://www.towersperrin .com/tillinghast/publications/reports/2003- Tort-Cos ts_Update/Tort_Costs-Trends- 2003_Update.pdf*.

54  Editorial, "Mr. Spitzer's Allies," *Wall Street Journal*, November 15, 2004.

## Counterpoint: On Balance, Lawsuits Benefit Society

55  *Zauderer v. Office of Disciplinary Counsel*, 481 U.S. 626, 643 (1985).

56  Feinman, *Law 101*, p. 135.

57  *Grimshaw v. Ford Motor Company*, 119 Cal. App. 3d 757, 810, 174 Cal. Rptr. 348, 382-8 (Cal. Ct. App. 1981).

58  Government Printing Office, *Report of the Senate Committee on Commerce, Science, and Transportation on S.648, the Product Liability Reform Act of 1997*. Washington, D.C.: Government Printing Office, 1997, pp. 76–77.

59  Editorial, "Vioxx: A Case Against Tort Reform," *St. Petersburg Times*, November 10, 2004.

60  Lisa Stansky, "Debate Tackles Legal Reforms," *New Orleans Times-Picayune*, October 8, 2004.

61  Jeffrey Robert White, "The Civil Jury: 200 Years Under Siege," 36 Trial 6, June 2000, 18.

62  Todd Smith, Letter to the Editor, *New York Times*, December 27, 2004.

63  *Greenman v. Yuba Power Products*, 59 Cal. 2d 57, 63, 377 P.2d 897, 901 (1963).

64  Feinman, *Law 101*, p. 90.

## Point: It Is Too Easy to Abuse the Legal System

65  Philip K. Howard, Testimony Before the House Judiciary Committee, June 22, 2004.

66  Olson, *Litigation Explosion*, p. 289.

67  Ibid., p. 107.

68  American Medical Association, *Medical Liability Reform—NOW!*. Chicago, IL: American Medical Association, 2004, p. 51. Available at *http://www.ama-assn.org/ama1/ pub/upload/mm/450/mlrnowdec032004 .pdf*.

69  Boot, *Out of Order*, p. 164.

70  Remarks by President Bush in a Conversa- tion on Asbestos Litigation, Clinton Town- ship, Michigan, January 7, 2005. Available at *http://www.whitehouse.gov/news/releases/ 2005/01/print/20050107-8.html*.

71  Hope Street Group, *Just Compensation* pp. 5–6. Available at *http://www.hopestreet- group.org/publications/Tort%20Reform .pdf*.

72 Marcia Coyle, "House Votes to Bring Bite Back to Rule 11," *National Law Journal*, September 27, 2004.

73 William Baldwin, "The Precarious Right to Speak the Truth," *Forbes*, August 16, 2004.

74 Stuart Taylor Thomas, "Civil Wars."

75 Boot, *Out of Order*, pp. 199–200.

**Counterpoint: Baseless Lawsuits Are the Exception, Not the Rule**

76 Stephanie Mencimer, "'Tort Reform' Lone Star Style," *Southern Exposure*, October 2004. Available at *http://www.southernstud-ies.org/reports/LoneStarTortReform.pdf*.

77 Nader and Smith, *No Contest*, p. 261.

78 Ibid., p. 275.

79 J. Russell Tyldesley, "The Real Goal of 'Tort Reform,'" *Baltimore Chronicle & Sentinel*, December 17, 2004. Available at *http://www.baltimorechronicle.com/121704Tyldesley.html*.

80 Joshua Green, "John Edwards, Esq.," *Washington Monthly*, October 2001.

81 Nader and Smith, *No Contest*, p. 118.

82 Elihu Inselbuch, "Contingent Fees and Tort Reform: A Reassessment and Reality Check," 64 Law & Contemp. Probs.2–3, Spring-Summer 2001, 175.

83 Council of State Governments, *Trends Alert: Medical Malpractice Crisis*. Lexington, KY: Council of State Governments, 2003, p. 8. Available at *http://www.csg.org/NR/rdonlyres/ek7ao3dfatxrcgh656amm6vnlw2o wndpku4rp3xhss32rzeche5ggb4j4mbw-dozh4zsobfboqxysz3bnp5corc6rrae/Medical+Malpractice+%28May+Revised %29.pdf*.

84 Foundation for Taxpayer and Consumer Rights news release, "Top Five Cases of Corporate Lawsuit Abuse Uncovered," September 15, 2004. Available at *http://www.consumerwatchdog.org/corporate/pr/pr004620.php3*.

**Conclusion: The Future of Tort Reform**

85 Public Law 109-2.

86 S. 2290, 108th Congress, the Fairness in Asbestos Injury Resolution (FAIR) Act of 2004.

87 H.R. 5, 108th Congress, the Help Efficient, Accessible, Low-Cost, Timely Healthcare (HEALTH) Act of 2003.

88 Rachel Zimmerman and Joseph T. Hallinan, "As Malpractice Caps Spread, Lawyers Turn Away Some Cases," *Wall Street Journal*, October 8, 2004.

89 §6, H.R. 4571, 108th Congress, the Lawsuit Abuse Reduction Act of 2004.

90 H.R. 339, 108th Congress, the Personal Responsibility in Food Consumption Act.

91 H.R. 1036, 108th Congress, the Protection of Lawful Commerce in Arms Act.

92 Tex. Civil Prac. & Rem. Code §41.003(a).

93 Nader and Smith, *No Contest*, p. 312.

94 Center for Justice and Democracy news release, "Center for Justice & Democracy Announces Hilarious 'Top 10 Zany Immunity Law Awards, 2004,'" December 13, 2004. Available at *http://www.centerjd.org/press/release/ZanyAwardRel.pdf*.

95 Jeffrey Robert White, "Mandatory Arbitration: A Growing Threat," 35 Trial 7, July 1999, 32.

96 Lindsay Fortado, "States Weigh Med-Mal Courts," *National Law Journal*, December 16, 2004.

## Books and Articles

American Medical Association. *Medical Liability Reform—NOW!* Chicago, IL: American Medical Association, 2004. Available at *http://www.ama-assn.org/ amal/pub/upload/mm/450/mirnowjunell2004.pdf.*

Americans for Insurance Reform. News Release: "Tillinghast's 'Tort Cost' Figures Vastly Overstate the Cost of American Legal System." Washington, D.C.: Americans for Insurance Reform, 2004. Available at *http://www.insurance-reform.org/pr/Tillinghast_Overstates.pdf.*

Boot, Max. *Out of Order: Arrogance, Corruption, and Incompetence on the Bench.* New York: Basic Books, 1998.

Bureau of Justice Statistics. *Civil Trial Cases and Verdicts in Large Counties, 2001.* Washington, D.C.: Bureau of Justice Statistics, 2004. Available at *http://www.ojp.usdoj.gov/bjs/pub/pdf/ctcvlc01.pdf.*

Manhattan Institute. *Trial Lawyers, Inc.: A Report on the Lawsuit Industry in America* 2003. New York: Manhattan Institute, Center for Legal Policy, 2003. Available at *http://www.manhattan-institute.org/triallawyersinc.pdf.*

Nader, Ralph, and Wesley J. Smith. *No Contest: Corporate Lawyers and the Perversion of Justice in America.* New York: Random House, 1996.

Olson, Walter K. *The Rule of Lawyers: How the New Litigation Elite Threatens America's Rule of Law.* New York: St. Martin's Press, 2003.

Tillinghast-Towers Perrin. *Trends and Findings on the Costs of the U.S. Tort System.* New York: Tillinghast-Towers Perrin, 2003. Available at *http://www.towersperrin.com/tillinghast/publications/reports/ 2003-Tort-Cos ts_Update/Tort_Costs-Trends-2003_Update.pdf.*

———.U.S. Tort Costs: *2004 Update. Trends and Findings on the Costs of the U.S. Tort System.* New York: Tillinghast-Towers Perrin, 2004. Available at *http://www.towersperrin.com/tillinghast/publications/reports/ Tort_2004/Tort.pdf.*

## Websites
### American Medical Association
*www.ama-assn.org*
This is the nation's largest doctors' organization. It takes a stand on legislative issues that involve health, including malpractice liability.

### American Tort Reform Association
*www.atra.org*
This is a broad-based coalition of more than 300 corporations, municipalities, and professional firms that support tort reform.

### Association of Trial Lawyers of America
*www.atla.org*
This is the nation's leading organization of plaintiffs' lawyers. It lobbies against tort reform at the national and state levels.

### Center for Justice and Democracy
*www.centerjd.org*
This public interest organization that educates Americans about the importance of jury trial and an independent judiciary.

### Common Good
*www.cgood.org*
This bipartisan organization advocates greater legal protection for health-care and education professionals.

### Consumer Federation of America
*www.consumerfed.org*
This coalition of 300 nonprofit organizations advocates the interests of consumers and the poor.

### Foundation for Taxpayer and Consumer Rights
*www.consumerwatchdog.org*
This California-based nonprofit education and advocacy organization specializes in the rights of health-care consumers.

### National Association of Manufacturers
*www.nam.org*
The nation's largest industrial trade association favors tort reform and the selection of pro-business judges.

### Public Citizen
*www.citizen.org*
This organization, founded by Ralph Nader in 1971, represents consumers' interests before Congress and federal agencies.

### United States Chamber of Commerce
*www.uschamber.org*
Founded in 1912, this organization represents American business. Its Litigation Center has participated in hundreds of cases.

## Cases

***Brown* v. *Kendall*,** 60 Mass. 292 (1850).
The ruling in this case held that a plaintiff in a tort case had to prove negligence on the part of the defendant in order to recover damages.

***Daubert* v. *Merrell Dow Pharmaceuticals, Inc.*,** 509 U.S. 579 (1993).
This case established a flexible standard for the admission of scientific testimony in federal trials. Reformers believe that this decision helped keep "junk science" out of the courtroom.

***Greenman* v. *Yuba Power Products*,** 59 Cal. 2d 57, 377 P.2d 897 (1963).
This case adopted the standard of strict-tort liability in defective-product cases.

***Grimshaw* v. *Ford Motor Company*,** 119 Cal. App. 3d 757, 174 Cal. Rptr. 348 (Cal. Ct. App. 1981).
The ruling in this case upheld an award of 3.5 million dollars in punitive damages against Ford, which allegedly marketed the Pinto despite knowing how dangerous it was.

***Palsgraf* v. *Long Island Railroad Company*,** 248 N.Y. 339, 162 N.E. 99 (1928).
The ruling in this case required that a plaintiff be within the "zone of danger" created by the defendant's negligence in order to recover damages.

***State Farm Mutual Automobile Insurance Company* v. *Campbell*,** 538 U.S. 408 (2003).
This case held that excessive punitive-damage awards were unconstitutional and that a punitive award more than four times the compensatory award would generally be considered excessive.

***World-Wide Volkswagen Corp.* v. *Woodson*,** 444 U.S. 286 (1980).
The ruling in this case stated that forcing an out-of-state defendant to defend a lawsuit was a violation of due process if the defendant lacked "minimum contacts" with that state.

## Legislation

**Cal. Civ. Code §3333.2.**
This statute, passed in 1975, limits noneconomic damages in a medical malpractice suit to $250,000. It is part of that state's Medical Injury Compensation Reform Act (MICRA).

**Michigan Court Rule 2.403.**
This rule authorizes judges to require the parties to submit their dispute to "case evaluation" before going to trial.

### Rule 11, Federal Rules of Civil Procedure.

This court rule authorized judges to fine lawyers who file frivolous lawsuits or otherwise abuse the legal system. Many state courts have similar rules.

### Rule 702, Federal Rules of Evidence.

This court rule requires a judge to conclude that expert testimony is reliable and scientifically valid before admitting it into evidence. Many state courts have similar rules.

### Section 402A, *Restatement (Second) of Torts.*

This codified the *Greenman* standard of strict-tort liability, which is now generally accepted by state courts.

### Texas Civ. Prac. & Remedies Code §§41.101 and following.

These code sections limit punitive-damage awards to $750,000 and set out criteria for awarding them.

### Texas Civ. Prac. & Remedies Code §§74.101 and following.

These code sections, part of a comprehensive medical malpractice-reform law, were passed in 2003. Their provisions include a cap on noneconomic damages and standards for expert testimony.

## Terms and Concepts

adversary system

alternative dispute resolution

appeal

civil procedure

class action

common law

contingent fee

damage cap

discovery

due process

expert testimony

"forum shopping"

frivolous litigation

immunity

"junk science"

lawsuit abuse

malpractice

mass tort

medical court

negligence

noneconomic damages

punitive damages

rules of procedure

SLAPP

strict liability

summary judgment

"tort tax"

## Beginning Legal Research

The goal of PoiNT/CounterPoint is not only to provide the reader with an introduction to a controversial issue affecting society, but also to encourage the reader to explore the issue more fully. This appendix, then, is meant to serve as a guide to the reader in researching the current state of the law as well as exploring some of the public-policy arguments as to why existing laws should be changed or new laws are needed.

Like many types of research, legal research has become much faster and more accessible with the invention of the Internet. This appendix discusses some of the best starting points, but of course "surfing the Net" will uncover endless additional sources of information—some more reliable than others. Some important sources of law are not yet available on the Internet, but these can generally be found at the larger public and university libraries. Librarians usually are happy to point patrons in the right direction.

The most important source of law in the United States is the Constitution. Originally enacted in 1787, the Constitution outlines the structure of our federal government and sets limits on the types of laws that the federal government and state governments can pass. Through the centuries, a number of amendments have been added to or changed in the Constitution, most notably the first ten amendments, known collectively as the Bill of Rights, which guarantee important civil liberties. Each state also has its own constitution, many of which are similar to the U.S. Constitution. It is important to be familiar with the U.S. Constitution because so many of our laws are affected by its requirements. State constitutions often provide protections of individual rights that are even stronger than those set forth in the U.S. Constitution.

Within the guidelines of the U.S. Constitution, Congress—both the House of Representatives and the Senate—passes bills that are either vetoed or signed into law by the President. After the passage of the law, it becomes part of the United States Code, which is the official compilation of federal laws. The state legislatures use a similar process, in which bills become law when signed by the state's governor. Each state has its own official set of laws, some of which are published by the state and some of which are published by commercial publishers. The U.S. Code and the state codes are an important source of legal research; generally, legislators make efforts to make the language of the law as clear as possible.

However, reading the text of a federal or state law generally provides only part of the picture. In the American system of government, after the legislature passes laws and the executive (U.S. President or state governor) signs them, it is up to the judicial branch of the government, the court system, to interpret the laws and decide whether they violate any provision of the Constitution. At the state level, each state's supreme court has the ultimate authority in determining what a law means and whether or not it violates the state constitution. However, the federal courts—headed by the U.S. Supreme Court—can review state laws and court decisions to determine whether they violate federal laws or the U.S. Constitution. For example, a state court may find that a particular criminal law is valid under the state's constitution, but a federal court may then review the state court's decision and determine that the law is invalid under the U.S. Constitution.

It is important, then, to read court decisions when doing legal research. The Constitution uses language that is intentionally very general—for example, prohibiting "unreasonable searches and seizures" by the police—and court cases often provide more guidance. For example, the U.S. Supreme Court's 2001 decision in *Kyllo* v. *United States* held that scanning the outside of a person's house using a heat sensor to determine whether the person is growing marijuana is unreasonable—*if* it is done without a search warrant secured from a judge. Supreme Court decisions provide the most definitive explanation of the law of the land, and it is therefore important to include these in research. Often, when the Supreme Court has not decided a case on a particular issue, a decision by a federal appeals court or a state supreme court can provide guidance; but just as laws and constitutions can vary from state to state, so can federal courts be split on a particular interpretation of federal law or the U.S. Constitution. For example, federal appeals courts in Louisiana and California may reach opposite conclusions in similar cases.

Lawyers and courts refer to statutes and court decisions through a formal system of citations. Use of these citations reveals which court made the decision (or which legislature passed the statute) and when and enables the reader to locate the statute or court case quickly in a law library. For example, the legendary Supreme Court case *Brown* v. *Board of Education* has the legal citation 347 U.S. 483 (1954). At a law library, this 1954 decision can be found on page 483 of volume 347 of the U.S. Reports, the official collection of the Supreme Court's decisions. Citations can also be helpful in locating court cases on the Internet.

Understanding the current state of the law leads only to a partial under-standing of the issues covered by the POINT/COUNTERPOINT series. For a fuller understanding of the issues, it is necessary to look at public-policy arguments that the current state of the law is not adequately addressing the issue. Many groups lobby for new legislation or changes to existing legislation; the National Rifle Association (NRA), for example, lobbies Congress and the state legislatures constantly to make existing gun control laws less restrictive and not to pass additional laws. The NRA and other groups dedicated to various causes might also intervene in pending court cases: a group such as Planned Parenthood might file a brief *amicus curiae* (as "a friend of the court")—called an "amicus brief"—in a lawsuit that could affect abortion rights. Interest groups also use the media to influence public opinion, issuing press releases and frequently appearing in interviews on news programs and talk shows. The books in POINT/COUNTERPOINT list some of the interest groups that are active in the issue at hand, but in each case there are countless other groups working at the local, state, and national levels. It is important to read everything with a critical eye, for sometimes interest groups present information in a way that can be read only to their advantage. The informed reader must always look for bias.

Finding sources of legal information on the Internet is relatively simple thanks to "portal" sites such as FindLaw (*www.findlaw.com*), which provides access to a variety of constitutions, statutes, court opinions, law review articles, news articles, and other resources—including all Supreme Court decisions issued since 1893. Other useful sources of information include the U.S. Government Printing Office (*www.gpo.gov*), which contains a complete copy of the U.S. Code, and the Library of Congress's THOMAS system (*thomas.loc.gov*), which offers access to bills pending before Congress as well as recently passed laws. Of course, the Internet changes every second of every day, so it is best to do some independent searching. Most cases, studies, and opinions that are cited or referred to in public debate can be found online— and *everything* can be found in one library or another.

The Internet can provide a basic understanding of most important legal issues, but not all sources can be found there. To find some documents it is necessary to visit the law library of a university or a public law library; some cities have public law libraries, and many library systems keep legal documents at the main branch. On the following page are some common citation forms.

//////////

# COMMON CITATION FORMS

| Source of Law | Sample Citation | Notes |
|---|---|---|
| **U.S. Supreme Court** | *Employment Division v. Smith,* 485 U.S. 660 (1988) | The U.S. Reports is the official record of Supreme Court decisions. There is also an unofficial Supreme Court ("S. Ct.") reporter. |
| **U.S. Court of Appeals** | *United States v. Lambert,* 695 F.2d 536 (11th Cir.1983) | Appellate cases appear in the Federal Reporter, designated by "F." The 11th Circuit has jurisdiction in Alabama, Florida, and Georgia. |
| **U.S. District Court** | *Carillon Importers, Ltd. v. Frank Pesce Group, Inc.,* 913 F.Supp. 1559 (S.D.Fla.1996) | Federal trial-level decisions are reported in the Federal Supplement ("F. Supp."). Some states have multiple federal districts; this case originated in the Southern District of Florida. |
| **U.S. Code** | Thomas Jefferson Commemoration Commission Act, 36 U.S.C., §149 (2002) | Sometimes the popular names of legislation—names with which the public may be familiar—are included with the U.S. Code citation. |
| **State Supreme Court** | *Sterling v. Cupp,* 290 Ore. 611, 614, 625 P.2d 123, 126 (1981) | The Oregon Supreme Court decision is reported in both the state's reporter and the Pacific regional reporter. |
| **State Statute** | Pennsylvania Abortion Control Act of 1982, 18 Pa. Cons. Stat. 3203-3220 (1990) | States use many different citation formats for their statutes. |

page:
   15: Associated Press, AP/Eric Draper
   48: Associated Press, AP/Joe Marquette
   61: Associated Press, AP/Rogelio Solis
   87: Associated Press, AP/David J. Phillip
  105: Associated Press, AP/Phil Coale

**PAUL RUSCHMANN, J.D.**, is a legal analyst and writer based in Canton, Michigan. He received his undergraduate degree from the University of Notre Dame and his law degree from the University of Michigan. He is a member of the State Bar of Michigan. His areas of specialization include legislation, public safety, traffic and transportation, and trade regulation. He is also the author of *Legalizing Marijuana, Mandatory Military Service, The War on Terror, The FCC and Regulating Indecency,* and *Media Bias,* other titles in the Point/Counterpoint series. He can be found on line at www.PaulRuschmann.com.

**ALAN MARZILLI, M.A., J.D.**, of Durham, North Carolina, is an independent consultant working on several ongoing projects for state and federal government agencies and nonprofit organizations. He has spoken about mental health issues in thirty states, the District of Columbia, and Puerto Rico; his work includes training mental health administrators, nonprofit management and staff, and people with mental illness and their family members on a wide variety of topics, including effective advocacy, community-based mental health services, and housing. He has written several handbooks and training curricula that are used nationally. He managed statewide and national mental health advocacy programs and worked for several public interest lobbying organizations in Washington, D.C., while studying law at Georgetown University.